. . . .

Ice Carving Made Easy

Second Edition

Ice Carving Made Easy

Second Edition

Joseph Amendola

JOHN WILEY & SONS, INC.

New York   Chichester   Weinheim   Brisbane   Singapore   Toronto

98 99 10 9 8 7

Library of Congress Cataloging-in-Publication Data

Amendola, Joseph.
   Ice carving made easy / Joseph Amendola.—2nd ed.
      p.   cm.
   Includes bibliographical references.
   ISBN 0-471-28570-6
   1. Ice carving—Technique.   I. Title.
NK6030.A55   194
736'.94—dc20   94-10129
                                                                                        CIP

Contents

Ice-Carving Associations and Manufacturers *115*

Acknowledgments

I would like to thank Steve Rose who provided photographs of carvings used in this manual, Karen Petroangelo for the illustrations, Tara Thomas for organizing and researching the history chapter, J.B. Prince Company, Inc. for the photographs of tools, Kanzo Tomori for his assistance with several carvings and photos, Michael d'Amore for his Chain Link carving and accompanying information, Daniel Hugelier for the photo and accompanying instruction for the Fan Centerpiece, the National Ice Carving Association for their help, and all the generous experts who gave their time and suggestions.

. . . .

Foreword
by Larry Malchik

*W*hen I enrolled at The Culinary Institute of America in 1975, Joseph Amendola's first edition of *Ice Carving Made Easy* was included in our basic set of books. Though ice carving was only briefly touched on in our two-year curriculum, that book was to be the introduction of one of the most meaningful activities of my life. The basics of ice carving that I learned, and then practiced on my own, following the drawings and photographs, opened up a world of opportunities and professional fulfillment that continue to unfold nearly two decades later. What began as a relatively simple artistic outlet grew to include elaborate designs, professional competition with my peers, enormous winter festival displays, exciting world travel, and a hand in the development of the National Ice Carving Association, all joys that I share with the thousands of students that Joe's books have launched onto similar paths.

With this new edition of *Ice Carving Made Easy,* Joe Amendola is sharing with all present and future ice carvers the resurgence of this historic art form that his initial book helped to spawn. Joe's personal dedication to instruction in the culinary arts has continued to educate and motivate chefs and artists in this unique medium. His work as ambassador to the culinary world has drawn together ice carvers from many countries, and here he shares the knowledge that we all need to continue expanding our skills. His selfless participation as a Certified Ice Carving Judge, his tireless help at the many national and international competitions, and his sincere desire to bring together the many personalities and associations for the benefit of culinarians young and old, define his position as the leading authority on the modern approach to ice carving.

I am sure this new edition of *Ice Carving Made Easy* will guide and inspire thousands more chefs and artists to enjoy the artistic fulfillment, professionalism, and camaraderie that I have realized from the exciting art of ice carving.

Larry Malchick
President, National Ice Carving Association

Foreword

by Hiroshi Noguchi

Joseph Amendola's contributions to the food and hospitality industry and the world of ice carving have earned him my admiration and respect and that of countless other colleagues and students as well.

About twenty years ago, I started ice carving after seeing my first ice carving chain saw. I was excited and full of ideas, but, needless to say, I could really have used this book at that time. The information Joe has compiled on the history, tools and accessories, different methods, types of ice blocks, and safety and precautionary measures in ice carving will be of tremendous help to many young enthusiasts in their goal to become professional ice sculptors.

Joe's association with The Culinary Institute of America and his extensive worldwide travel as a food and hospitality consultant have awarded him the opportunity to gain important knowledge in the world of ice carving. Joe is always there to help the younger generation and to give them the guidelines and the inspiration. He is a good leader and is always looking forward to new concepts—I like that in him. I believe that this new book will encourage beginning carvers with its new ideas and provide them with unique challenges in the world of ice carving.

I look forward to following in Joe's footsteps by contributing to the wonderful and exciting world of ice sculpture for many years to come. My sincere congratulations to Joe, and I wish him much success with this new book.

Hiroshi Noguchi, C.E.C., A.A.C
Executive Chef
Stouffer Orlando Resort

. . . .

Preface

*T*his revision of *Ice Carving Made Easy* is intended to combine some old ideas with new innovations in the ice carving profession.

Ice carving has become more and more popular over the years. Original ice art has enhanced many lavish affairs as well as numerous intimate ones. Carvings add to the festivity and individuality of the affair with their grace and fantasy.

I would like to acknowledge the help and support given freely by my friends and colleagues, and the many graduates who have helped make my career a very happy and interesting one.

I have been associated with The Culinary Institute of America since its inception in the 1940s, serving in various capacities: instructor, V.P. of faculty, Dean of Students, V.P. Student Affairs, Acting President, and most recently as Ambassador.

I have travelled extensively as a food and hospitality consultant worldwide. I now reside in Orlando, Florida and am involved as a partner with Fessel International Hospitality with offices in Orlando, California, Zürich and Tokyo.

I hope this revised edition of *Ice Carving Made Easy* will be as interesting and rewarding to those who read it, as it was for me to write it.

Joseph Amendola

Joseph Amendola

Chapter *1*

. . . .

The History of Ice Carving

The earliest known record of an ice harvest is found in the *Shih cheng,* or "Book of Songs," written sometime after 600 B.C. This collection of ballads and stories describes the everyday life of the Shensi warrior-farmers as they lived in the highlands of northwest China, and mentions their winter routine of flooding their fields with water. When the water had frozen, the ice was cut into blocks and stored in icehouses. Ice stored here kept cool through evaporation. Large quantities of straw were used as insulation. The ice was used in the warmer months to keep their fish fresh. In other iceless places, ice was carted from cooler areas, usually the peaks of the nearest mountain range, by relays of men on horseback.

In the Third Century B.C., a Chinese poem shows expanded interest in the use of ice—iced drinks. "The Summons of the Soul" lists "all kinds of good food," including "ice-cooled liquor, strained of impurities, clear wine, cool and refreshing." It seems the treat was enjoyed so much that people overindulged: Hippocrates, in the Fourth Century B.C., reported that "most men would rather run the hazard of their lives or health than be deprived the pleasures of drinking out of ice."

Heedless of his warning, Aristotle was teaching people to make ice from snow by plunging a hot object into it to make part of it melt, and watching it refreeze as ice when the object was removed. His pupil, Alexander the Great, learned to appreciate ice so much that, as ruler, he had trenches dug and filled with snow and ice from the nearby mountains in which to cool his kegs of wine. By the First Century A.D., the Roman Emperor Nero had developed a taste for ice mixed with fruit juices, an early precursor of today's sorbet. In India too, relays would rush ice from the mountains of Hinku Kush to Delhi for the aristocracy to enjoy plain or mixed with juices.

Though it is widely believed that Marco Polo, during his travels in China in the 1200s, observed the Chinese mixing saltpeter (rocksalt) with ice to lower its freezing point, there is no evidence to support this claim. It is more likely that this technique was not discovered until sometime in the late 1500s in Italy.

It was a monumental discovery, for this would allow the molding of ice into amusing and pretty forms. Though copious amounts of chipped or block ice had been used on the buffet to keep foods chilled, this marked the first use of ice sculpture on the table. The presence of sugars makes freezing more difficult, so it was another one hundred years before effective methods for freezing fruit syrups and creams was figured out. Prior to this, the iced mixtures people ate were much more like slush than what we would call ice cream.

Legend also has it that news of this delicacy reached France in 1533, when Catherine de Medici, a Florentine, married the soon-to-be Henry the II, King of France, and brought her brigade of cooks to Paris. This story is undocumented and improbable; her death in 1589 preceded the discovery of the ice and salt connection. At any rate, iced delicacies became quite popular among the aristocrats in Italy in the 1600s, and soon caught on in France. In 1670, the first café in Paris to sell ices and possibly ice creams was opened by Francisco Procopio, (known in France as Procope), a Sicilian. By 1676, there were 250 "limonadiers," as these ice makers were called, in the city.

By the 1700s, ice pits were so common in Italy that The Encyclopedia Britannica, in 1771, reported that "the meanest person in Italy who rents a house has his vault or cellar for ice." An account recorded by the British scientist Robert Boyle (1624–1691) describes the pits. Usually located in the cool shadows at the foot of the mountain, the opening was generally 25 feet across, protected by a tent-like thatched roof with a narrow door on one side. This led into a room fifty feet deep. Wooden planks covered the sides and a wooden grate covered with clean straw was placed at the base for drainage. Snow would be beaten into layers one foot thick, divided by clean straw to make removal in the spring easier. Soon ice pits patterned after these appeared all across Europe.

The Ice Trade

The trade of ice quickly became an important source of revenue for many countries, as those without cold seasons and mountains looked to other countries with these resources. Constantinople relied heavily on Bursa, in the mountains of Turkey, and Egypt received ice from Syria. The Spanish Sierra Nevadas supplied ice to the city of Oran, Algeria, and men on horseback in Lima, Peru made a thirty-six hour trek to retrieve ice from the Andes, a trip that lost up to one-third of it from melting. The success of these trips depended solely on speed and insulating layers of straw, leaves, and furs.

There were ways to avoid this inconvenience in areas where the temperature dropped very low at night: European colonists in Allahabad, India would set out hundreds of shallow pans on a raised bed of earth which they filled with water in the evening. At three AM, the servants would chip out the ice that had formed and pack it tightly in the ice houses. A report written by a member of the Light Bengal Artillery recorded that up to three thousand pounds of ice could be collected each night from a 20-acre field. When the pits were filled, they were closed up until April 1, the customary day to begin deliveries.

In the 1800s, Americans realized the potential of New England's ice resources and began large-scale export out of Boston. In 1806, Frederick Tudor (1783–1864), a Bostonian widely known as the "Ice King," was the first to ship ice to the West Indies. An outbreak of yellow fever in Martinique that year created great demand for ice to help lower the dangerously high body temperatures of those with the disease.

Although the venture was a financial disaster due to excessive loss by melting, it established Tudor's business. He went on to dominate the industry until the 1850s. By 1816 he had built an ice house in Havana, Cuba that held up to 150 tons of ice, which secured his monopoly on the trade to both Havana and Jamaica. In May 1833, he was shipping as far as Calcutta. It was at this time that he began designing ice boxes for the home. They became a standard until the electric refrigerator replaced them in the early 1940s. By 1845, Boston was shipping 156,540 tons of ice each season. Eleven years later, Tudor's trade had grown to include Liverpool, Bombay, and the major ports of South America.

Ice Harvesting

The harvesting of ice was arduous and dangerous work. It was always done as quickly as possible to avoid a sudden warm spell and to secure the cut ice: ice blocks cut in the morning that remained in the water would freeze back together by the end of the day.

As soon as the ice was thick enough, a horse-drawn ice plane was used to remove the rough, porous surface ice and any accumulation of snow. Standing snow was removed repeatedly because snow would insulate the ice and prevent it from becoming any thicker.

In the early 1800s, men would first mark the ice into rectangles by means of a guide-plow directed by a tight cord. Next, the ice would be cut into blocks by hand using large, heavy crosscut saws. The blocks had to be lifted from the water with ice tongs or pulled out by horses fitted with steel-cleated horseshoes.

Later, new tools sped the process considerably, allowing the industry to expand from a cottage business to a full-scale industry. The inventions of Bostonian Nathanial Jarvis Wyeth (1802–1856) stand out particularly. Wyeth, the manager of the Fresh Pond Hotel in Massachusetts, was interested in finding more efficient ice harvesting methods to speed the filling of the hotel's ice house. His 1825 invention of a cutter with double saw-toothed blades improved the process so much that he was made the exclusive supplier of ice to Mr. Tudor for many years.

Rather than having to mark out each line carefully on the ice with the guide-plow, the new ice cutter cut two specifically-spaced parallel lines at a time. Half as many passes across the ice were needed to complete the marking of uniformly-sized ice blocks. The grooves it left were then cut deeper with a "swingcutter," and snow and ice chips were packed into them with long, chisel-ended calking bars to prevent the blocks from freezing together. The two outside rows were then sawed off with a heavy handsaw, and the next knocked off with chisel bars. Rough edges were removed with a hatchet when the ice was removed from the water. The blocks were lifted out onto the ice sheet with the aid of hook-picks or, when possible, floated down the river to the ice house. If floated, the blocks would be guided by men on shore with 16- to 20-foot-long hooked poles, or, where this was impossible, by men standing on them, poling them down the waterway. Often, though, the ice was loaded directly onto horse-drawn sleighs for immediate delivery to ice houses. Major ice houses were located close to the shore and used steam-powered conveyor belts to transport the ice from shore to house. Inside the house, men would quickly stack the blocks in neat rows, chiseling them to fit perfectly.

Although this industry provided a great source of revenue for many towns, both through the money earned in the sale of ice and the influx of outsiders seeking employment, it was dangerous to the men and horses that worked the ice. It was not uncommon for either to slip and fall into the icy water. More importantly, an increasing problem was that of sanitation; the waterways were becoming more polluted—not to mention what happens when there are 100 horses working the ice. These factors, combined with the increased demand for alternate means of refrigeration precipitated by the Industrial Revolution's population and transportation boom, necessitated the invention of alternative methods of procuring ice.

Early Ice Manufacturing

In 1834, an American from Newburyport, Massachusetts living in England, Jacob Perkins (1796–1884), obtained a British patent for the first ice-making machine. It functioned on the same principle as our refrigerators do today, except it used ether, which is much less efficient than the extremely volatile Freon used today. The following years saw a number of unsuccessful ice machines patented in the United States and England, until in 1859 Ferdinand Carré presented an ice machine that employed ammonia, a much more volatile (and therefore efficient) liquid than ether, that made it feasible to run a large-scale ice factory. A plant based on this cooling technique was developed in the South, where ice could cost up to an exorbitant seventy-five dollars a ton, due to transportation costs and risk of melting involved, as compared to two dollars a ton in the Northeast. A small experimental ice plant opened in New Orleans in 1864, producing up to 200 pounds of ice per hour. By 1868, it had become a full-sized operation, regularly producing 60 tons a day. Sixty-nine years later, there were 49 plants in New Orleans alone.

Today, a typical ice plant can produce approximately 600 tons of ice each day. Most of the ice is needed by restaurants, hotels, and hospitals for the cooling of foods and the icing of beverages. Much is used for shipping of foodstuffs, or for the preservation of other temperature-sensitive materials, such as certain types of photographic film. Some is distributed to stores to be sold to customers for home use. A small percentage is made expressly for ice carving.

Average ice is produced by lowering large containers of water into tanks filled with brine held at 15 degrees Fahrenheit and cooled by ammonia. The calcium chloride of the brine acts as a temper to prevent the brine from freezing. The containers freeze in 24 hours, and the ice is broken up according to the manner in which it will be used.

Ice for ice carving is produced in a similar manner in large ice-producing plants, except that air is bubbled into the container as the water freezes, helping to equalize the temperature throughout and extract the impurities that would cloud the ice. This air is the reason for the cloudy column left in the center of a block of carving ice; this very last bit of water does not receive the benefits of the agitation. With proper tempering, ice produced by this method possesses superior pliability to natural ice because it lacks weaknesses caused by irregularities.

Early Beginnings of Ice Carving

Even without these technological advances, ice carving had been flourishing in snow-bound countries for centuries. Of course, the Eskimos have long used their icy climate to greatest advantage—building homes of packed snow and ice impermeable to the biting wind and bitter coldness. But the first records of the building and sculpting of ice for pure pleasure and entertainment point to Russia as the major early center of this art.

Every year began on New Year's Day with a ritual chasing away of evil spirits involving an ice sculpture: blocks of ice would be taken from a lake to build a large ice cross, and the spirits would be whisked away down the hole left in the ice. Celebrations such as "Maslenitsa," the Russian equivalent of Shrovetide, presented an opportunity to create ice and snow sculptures to both entertain and commemorate the pagan god of winter of the same name.

Russian winter festivals seem to have grown in scale with the grandness of the empire. In 1739, an immense ice palace was commissioned by Empress Anna Ivanova, daughter of Peter the Great. The winter was one of the harshest on record, and the palace was to furnish a diversion for the people, as well as provide the site of an outrageous "joke." Disgruntled with Prince Dmitrii Golitsyn, the Empress had forced him to marry her ugliest servant, a woman she nicknamed "Buzhenina" after a dish of roast pork sauced in spiced vinegar and onions. The prince was to spend his wedding night in the palace.

The imperial architect Eropkin outdid himself: he created a Palladian palace on the banks of the Neva in St. Petersburg measuring more than 21 feet high and 54 feet long by 17½ feet wide. The ice, harvested from the Neva, was said to have been exceptionally clear and blue, and the walls were finished with water so that the junctions between blocks were not detectable. Window frames, doors, and pillars were painted to look like green marble. Windows were made from extraordinarily thin ice that was backlit at night by candles. They looked out over an ice balustrade that surrounded the palace, and ice birds perched in 29 ice trees that were tinted to look realistic. Six statues and an elaborate frontispiece graced the front entrance; two dolphin fountains and one life-sized elephant fountain sprayed water 24 feet into the air. Two mortars and six cannons fashioned of ice were working replicas; they fired frequently. An ice-log bathhouse, also functional and used on occasion, completed the grounds.

Inside, every detail was carved from ice. The highlight was a translucent clock with all of its interior mechanisms detailed, displayed on an ice table in the middle of the drawing room. Two ball-footed benches pressed up against opposite walls. A corner cupboard was filled with a tea service, cups, glasses, and colored replicas of plated dishes. The bedroom contained a large canopied bed with a mattress, quilt, and two pillows, each with nightcaps laid out on them, all made of ice. To the side stood a bedside table and stool upon which two pairs of slippers rested. Across the room was a fireplace filled with logs and a dressing table ornamented with small bottles, trinket boxes, and two candlesticks. The candles and logs in the fireplace were sometimes doused with petroleum and lit for show. The ice mirror on the wall sparkled in the flames' light. This was the newlywed couple's honeymoon suite.

The event surely amused, as well as made certain that the Prince was aware of Anna's displeasure with him. The married couple did survive, and the castle was dismantled and the ice deposited in the Imperial Palace's ice cellars.

This was the beginning of ice carving on the grandest of scales. Supposedly, in 1734 an even larger ice castle was commissioned for St. Petersburg by Empress Elizabeth, but it is poorly documented. The transience of ice seems to have discouraged the keeping of detailed records after the first palace was completed; unless the structures attracted enough interest to be written about, they melted and faded out of memory.

It was more than a century later, in 1883, that people began creating ice palaces in North America. The first structure was part of the First Annual Winter Carnival in Montreal, Canada, an event begun by the Montreal Snowshoe Club to attract tourists and celebrate the joys of their snowy winters. The seasoned architect A. C. Hutchinson of the Montreal firm Hutchinson and Steele designed the palace, and his brother J. H. Hutchinson headed the 50-person construction crew. Together they created a 90-square-foot castle from 500-pound blocks of ice. Four corner towers surrounded the 21-foot central tower. The roof was made of icicle-covered wooden beams and boughs. At dusk the palace was illuminated with electric light, a truly impressive sight considering that electric lighting was still quite new. The carnival was very successful, attracting about 15,000 tourists and receiving front-page coverage in newspapers such as *The New York Times.* The castle was the highlight of the event, and each year the goal was to create a bigger and more complex castle than the last.

A quarantine necessitated by a smallpox epidemic that hit the city in 1885–1886 caused the cancellation of the carnival that winter. The city of St. Paul, Minnesota took advantage of the opportunity and hired A. C. Hutchinson to design an ice palace for their first annual winter carnival. This festival, too, grew in size in the following years, featuring larger palaces and more decorative and numerous sculptures. Poor weather conditions in the winter of 1889 proved fatal to both the ice castles and winter events of the Montreal and St. Paul festivals, and put an end to both for several years.

Ottawa revived the creation of ice castles in 1895. Ice blocks taken from the Rideau River were provided for only the main portion of the building. The center tower was constructed instead of wood and cedar bows coated with ice, which made for an impressive torching of the castle at the end of the festival.

On January 1, 1896, the mining town of Leadville, Colorado, held an ice carnival to help stimulate the lagging local economy. The "Crystal Palace" that was the highlight of the event housed a skating rink and two ballrooms. The Fort Dodge Cowboy band provided live music from the balcony. Statues surrounding the palace depicted the life of miners, and a 31-foot statue of a woman, with her arm pointing to the rich mineral hills that had helped to make the town prosperous, greeted people at the northern entrance to the building. Unluckily, the festival did not attract the crowd it had hoped for, and the event was never repeated.

Meanwhile, the annual pre-Lent carnival in Quebec City had been growing in size since its beginnings in 1880. Simple colored snow statues were evolving into more elaborate sculptures carved by experienced artisans. 1894 saw the creation of an ice fortress standing 63 feet high and 120 feet long by 50 feet wide, a host of statues carved by experienced wood carver Louis Jobin, and a 50-foot beer bottle made of ice blocks. Two years later the castle was even more impressive, standing 37 feet higher with a spiral staircase circling it.

Ice sculpting was not limited to festivals. In 1904, and Ottawan called Constable Carey single-handedly constructed a fortress on the Governor General's front lawn in Quebec. The structure, 20 feet high and 40 feet long by 30 feet wide, was modeled after Castle Antrim in Ireland. He managed to complete it in two weeks.

Meanwhile, ice sculpting had been developing on a smaller scale in the dining room. By the Middle Ages, dinner had evolved into something much more complex than just eating; dining was a form of entertainment and an opportunity to display one's wealth. Tables became known as "groaning boards," referring to the weight of the excessive displays of food crowded in the center of the dining table. Edible and inedible decorative pieces, known as "soltelties," added to the spectacle, displayed on both the main table and on side tables all around the room. Their creation was the responsibility of the chef, so it is no surprise that sugar, butter, marzipan, pastry dough, and ice were the major materials used. The structures were usually human or architectural in form, and the level of detail and complexity such pieces demanded required a high degree of artistic prowess. In fact, in Italy, chefs were considered artists, and many esteemed artists dabbled in culinary decoration. Ice soon was recognized for much more than its chilling properties; its strength (comparable to that of concrete), resiliency, and light-reflecting translucency made for sturdy and dazzling ornaments.

In the early 1800s, the celebrated French chef and pâtissier Marie-Antoine Carême (1783–1833) raised culinary decoration to its highest level. Fascinated with architecture, Carême studied architectural drawings in the print room of the National Library in Paris, and based his creations on these. He came to believe that architecture was best exhibited in confectionery, and created large, ornamental confections displaying his belief. These pieces, known as "pièces montées" used many different materials, including ice.

The advent of Russian service in the late 1800s intensified the desire for table decorations. Since this style of service required that all of the courses were plated in the kitchen, the center of the dining table was left bare. Ice sculptures could decorate this area and provide a focus and conversation piece between courses. Ice sculptures also began to be incorporated into the actual dishes. Master chef Auguste Escoffier (1847–1935) became famous for his "Pêches Melba," created in 1892 while he was chef at the Savoy in London. The original dessert consisted of an ice swan that cradled on its back a scoop of ice cream topped with poached peaches and spun sugar, created in honor of Madame Nellie Melba, who had played Elsa in the opera Lohengrin, in which a swan figures prominently. Escoffier's "Suprême de Volailles Jeanette" also incorporated ice sculpture: a cold, stuffed breast of chicken was served on a ship carved out of ice. The dish was created to commemorate the collision of the ship Jeanette with an iceberg.

In the United States, ice sculpture in the dining room focused on the presentation of ice creams, a dessert that has always enjoyed fantastic popularity among Americans. Ice cream was introduced to America in the late 1700s by Thomas Jefferson, who was enthralled with all things French after serving as Minister to France from 1785–1789. By 1867, the restaurant Delmonico's in New York City was serving "sorbet à l'américaine" to celebrities like Charles Dickens. The dish consisted of "glasses" of ice filled with lemon, orange, champagne, kirsch, or prunelle sorbet, which were served as a palate cleanser between courses. These "glasses" were to become very popular; by the 1900s, ice cream served in "amusing forms" resting upon spun sugar bases were a standard children's birthday item. These forms were made with the wildly popular and diverse ice cream molds now available from caterers and mold manufacturers. Of course, they could also be filled with plain water, for the homemaker who wanted to impress guests with an ice sculpture.

Heckmann and Schlev's book *Artistic Sugar Work and Ice Sculpting* is a wonderful source of the applications of ice to dessert items that were popular in the early 1900s. Suggestions range from decoratively notching a piece of ice for use as a serving dish to creating an ice bowl with a handle of pulled caramel or a carved ice vase filled with pink caramel roses.

Fancy Ice Carving in Thirty Lessons, the 1947 lesson book for ice carvers by August Forster, shows a thorough understanding of ice carving history. His fruit salad baskets and relish, canape, and caviar containers are amazingly reminiscent of early buffet pieces. The gondolas and cornucopias for appetizers remind the reader of Carême's pièces montées, and his sailboats to serve fish follow Escoffier's example. Centerpieces of animals are the most numerous sculptures in his book, and trophies, letters, and numbers are suggested for all sorts of occasions. Small electric light bulbs and a coating of colored water or powdered chocolate, flour, or silver or gold dust are suggested to heighten the visual impact.

Ice carving was introduced rather late to Japan, but its advent there marked a new level of ice carving artistry. It was introduced by a Japanese chef, Tokuzo Akiyama, who told of the ice boats filled with fruit and small ice swans filled with sherbet he observed in France during a trip around 1917. The art did not become popular until after World War II, when the proliferation of refrigerators lowered the demand for ice and prompted the ice manufacturers to sponsor ice-carving competitions in an effort to revive the industry. The teacher and sculptor Shuko Kobayashi, the first chairman of the Japan Ice Sculpture Association, chaired the first annual competition in Tokyo in 1955. Eventually, a permanent school of ice carving was established in Tokyo, and the plethora of hotels with banquet facilities provided the perfect opportunity to produce large-scale works and to search for new presentation and decoration ideas. Each hotel soon hired its own carving specialists to keep up with the demand for quality and quantity.

The Japanese sensitivity to balance and detail and their familiarity with ice catapulted them to the forefront in ice carving. This mastery of ice art is best displayed in the annual Snow Festival every February in Sapporo, the capital of Hokkaido, Japan. The festival was started in 1950 with seven snow sculptures constructed by students from six high schools. By 1968, 150 sculptures were displayed to a crowd of 3,900,000 people. Today, families gather in Odori Park to create large ice and snow sculptures alongside army teams and professionals displaying their skills in this week-long celebration of winter. The result is a winter wonderland in which visitors are free to roam and play. Past attractions have included detailed miniature cities, replicas of the Statue of Liberty and the White House, and a huge cat whose tongue was a slide.

Today, ice sculptures are featured in festivals, competitions, and culinary events all over the world. They have even been part of political affairs: for a 1982 UNESCO conference, the Californian artist Joyce Cutler–Shaw carved in two-foot-high letters the word survival, which was placed in the United Nations Plaza. Water gathered from many different nations was poured over the ice, and when it melted, the mingled waters were placed in the United Nations' permanent collection.

Ice sculptures also have been employed in movies and advertisements, which demonstrates the power they possess to attract attention and impress. The 1940 movie Citizen Kane used the display of an ice carving at an upper-class party to symbolize the ice-cold treatment the party giver gave his employees. Ice played a more fantastic role in Edward Scissorhands: Edward painstakingly created a huge ice statue of the woman he loved, creating snow with the flecks of ice that flew off as he cut.

Ice carving's most dramatic role seems still to be fixed in winter festivals. Ice palaces and sculpture contests still provide a much-needed reprieve from long, cold winters, and provide people with an outlet for their urge to continue creating bigger more exotic sculptures every year. Guinness records for the world's largest snowman, the largest palace and the biggest man-made snow pile illustrate the ever-present challenge humans feel continually to make everything bigger and better. The degree of excellence achieved by professional sculptors in competitions today proves this urge. Viewing the complexity and quality of the sculptures of the Japanese who, as of this writing, hold first and second place in the world, it is impossible even to imagine what will be created in next year's world championship, but it is certain that ice sculpting has come a great distance since the days of the first snowball.

Bibliography

Amendola, Joseph. *Ice Carving Made Easy.* Washington, D.C.: National Restaurant Association. 1960.
Anderes, Fred, and Ann Agranoff. *Ice Palaces.* New York: Abbeville Press. 1983.

Bugialli, Giuliano. *Classic Techniques of Italian Cooking.* New York: Simon and Schuster/Fireside. 1989.

Chase's Annual Events, 1992. Chicago: Contemporary Books. 1991.

Clair, Colin. *Kitchen and Table.* London, New York, Toronto: Abelard-Schuman. 1964.

Cosman, Madeleine Pelner. *Fabulous Feasts: Medieval Cooking and Ceremony.* New York: George Brazilier. 1976.

David, Elizabeth. *Italian Food.* New York: Harper and Row. 1987.

Dingle, John. *International Chef.* New York: E. P. Dutton and Company, Inc. 1955.

Durocher, Joseph F. *Practical Ice Carving.* Boston: CBI Publishing Company, Inc. 1981.

Ellis, Monica. *Ice and Icehouses Through the Ages.* Southhampton, England: Southhampton University Industrial Archaeological Group. 1982.

Finance, Charles, *Buffet Catering.* New York: Ahrens Publishing Company, Inc. 1958.

Forster, August. *Fancy Ice Carving in Thirty Lessons.* Chicago: Northwestern Printing House. 1947.

Hamp, Pierre. *Kitchen Prelude (Mes Metiers).* New York: E. P. Dutton and Company, Inc. 1933.

Hasegwa, Hideo. *Ice Carving.* Carlsbad, California: Continental Publishing, Ltd. 1974.

Heckmann, A. and Albert Schlev. *Artistic Sugar Work and Ice Sculpting.* Nordhausen, Germany: Heinrich Killinger. 1925.

MacDonald Margaret Read, ed. *The Folklore of World Holidays.* Detroit/London: Gale Research Inc. 1992.

Mariani, John F. *The Dictionary of American Food and Drink.* New York: Tichnor and Fields. 1983.

Matsuo, Yukio. *Ice Sculpting Secrets of a Japanese Master.* New York: John Wiley and Sons, Inc. 1992.

Mennel, Stephen. *All Manners of Food.* Oxford, England: Basil Blackwell Ltd. 1985.

Montagne, Prosper. *Larousse Gastronomique.* New York: Crown Publishers Inc. 1984.

Morris, Helen, *Portrait of a Chef: the Life of Alexis Soyer.* New York: Macmillan Company. 1938.

Schmidt, Arno. *The Banquet Business, 2nd edition.* New York: Van Nostrand Reinhold. 1990.

Smith, Georgiana Reynolds. *Table Decoration Yesterday, Today, and Tomorrow.* Rutland, Vermont/Tokyo, Japan: Charles E. Tuttle Company. 1968.

Soyer, Alexis. *The Pantropheon.* New York/London: Paddington Press Ltd. 1977.

Tannahill, Reay. *Food in History.* New York: Stein and Day. 1973.

Visser, Margaret. *The Rituals of Dinner: The Origins, Evolution, Eccentricities and Means of Table Manners.* New York: Grove Weidenfeld. 1991.

Wheaton, Barbara Ketcham. *Ices Plain and Fancy.* New York: Metropolitan Museum of Art. 1976.

Wheaton, Barbara Ketcham. *Savoring the Past.* Philadelphia: University of Pennsylvania Press. 1983.

Chapter *2*
. . . .

Opportunities for Ice Carvers

Opportunities for Ice Carvers

A party isn't a party unless it features an ice carving! This sentiment is echoed by thousands of hosts and hostesses.

Ice carving can be fun. It can also be profitable. A skilled ice sculptor can usually get a good job in the catering department of a hotel, restaurant, or club, or with an ice-manufacturing firm.

The hotel, restaurant or club that offers a good selection of ice sculptures for social events has a distinct advantage over its competitors. In fact, this book may prove a valuable sales-promotion aid in selling carvings—the Banquet Manager can show customers the pictures as samples to consider, especially those in Chapters 5 and 10.

Extra money can also be earned from freelance jobs. The simplest carving may sell for $100 while more elaborate ones, such as the swan, lovebirds, or snowman may bring as much as several hundred.

Opportunities for selling ice carvings extend throughout the year. You may use Cupid at a summer wedding or to ring in the New Year; Santa Claus appears at Christmas time; and a flag on the Fourth of July. The possibilities are endless.

Here is a sample social calendar with carvings that may be featured at each occasion:

New Year: Cupid or horn of plenty

St. Valentine's day: Cupid or lovebirds on a heart

Easter: Rabbits, chickens, ducklings, etc.

Fourth of July: Patriotic symbols, silhouettes

Children's parties: Animals and birds of all sorts

Engagement parties, showers, weddings: Cupid on a heart or bell, bluebird of happiness, lovebirds on a heart or bell, or the initials of the bride and groom

Confirmation or bar mitzvah parties: Appropriate religious symbols, a Bible or Torah, or the initials of the person being honored

College functions: School insignia, Greek letters for fraternities

Sporting events and races: Boats, cars, submarines, horses, pennants, dogs, fish, yacht club burgees; symbols for football, baseball, basketball, hockey, boxing, skating, swimming; the school mascot (such as the Princeton tiger or the Yale bulldog), and so forth

Testimonial dinners and convention banquets: Ice silhouettes, reproductions of company trademarks, monograms, numerals for years, a replica of the product made or symbol of the honored person's accomplishments or hobby (such as a harp for music, palette and brushes for art, etc.)

Thanksgiving: Turkey or horn of plenty

Christmas: Santa Claus, choir of angels, carolers, Christmas tree bedecked with small colored balls, candles, candelabra, cornucopia, bluebird of happiness, reindeer drawing a sleigh (with may be decorated with a winter bouquet, a ready-made figure of Santa, or a stack of attractively wrapped boxes). A really ambitious sculptor might even do a crèche populated with ready-made figures of angels, shepherds, wise men, and sheep.

Hannukah: Menorah

Too many carvings to do for the same date? Ice can be sculpted months ahead and stored at the local ice house or in a freezer while awaiting the occasions at which it will be featured.

National Ice Carving Association

The National Ice Carving Association is an organization that promotes the art of ice sculpture through education, competitions, standardized judging, and exhibitions. NICA sanctions ice carving exhibitions and competitions throughout the United States.

NICA competitions are judged on the basis of a uniform set of criteria developed and reviewed annually by NICA's Board of Directors. Standards include: design and composition, creativity, overall impression and technical skill. All judges of NICA-sanctioned events must first be certified by the NICA Judging Committee. Judging applications are available to all members.

NICA publishes a newsletter giving general information on ice-carving techniques and dates and cities of scheduled ice-carving competitions.

Additional information can be obtained by writing NICA, see the list of associations and manufacturers.

Chapter 3
....

Tools & Accessories

Basic Power Tools and Hand Tools

With a few basic tools, you can complete most of the carvings illustrated in this book. I've also illustrated other tools needed for more advanced work. A full knowledge of all tools will lead to faster carving and more detailed, professional presentation.

Various types of chisels, as shown in Figure 3–8, are used for detail work:

1. 1-inch bent gouge;

2. 7/8-inch V-shape;

3. 1 1/4-inch gouge;

4. 2-inch straight;

5. 1 1/2-inch straight;

6. 1 1/4-inch straight;

7. 5/8-inch straight.

Many different types of chisels are available, with wooden handles of various lengths, depending on the level of detail of your carving.

FIGURE 3–1 Gasoline or **Electric Chain Saw** Used to cut and shape ice.

FIGURE 3–2 Die Grinder Bit accessories are available for detailing and drawing on the carving.

FIGURE 3–3 Heat Gun Used for glossing, rounding, and repairing.

FIGURE 3–4 Ice Tongs Used to move large ice blocks.

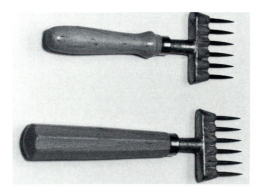

FIGURE 3–5 Ice Chipper Used to shave, rough out forms, and scribe a design into the ice.

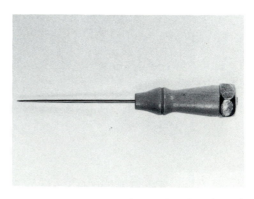

FIGURE 3–6 Ice Pick Used to break and cut large pieces of ice from a block.

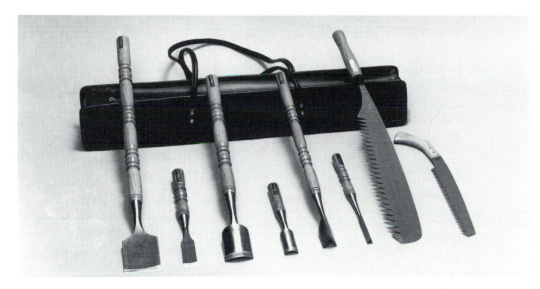

FIGURE 3–7 **Chisels** and **Hand Saws** The tools shown address the basic needs of both professional and beginner carvers.

FIGURE 3–8 **Chisels** A variety of shapes and types of chisels used for detail work.

Steam Cutting of Ice

The steam-cutting method was popular years ago when steam facilities were widely available in hotels. As other more versatile techniques for cutting ice were adopted, the hotel facilities for steam cutting were largely discontinued.

The steam-cutting method is somewhat inconvenient; you must have access to live steam and you are limited to a specific location for the ice cutting. If you use this method, the procedure is as follows: connect the steam hose to the boiler; attach the steam gun with copper tubing; when you are ready, depress the lever on the steam valve, which will allow live steam through the copper tubing. This tubing will act as a cutting edge.

This method is rather slow, but is still preferred by some carvers accustomed to older techniques. To my knowledge, there is currently no company that sells this equipment as a whole. It may be easily assembled by a plumber or someone versed in plumbing techniques.

Two New Tools

These two new tools, the Percival (shown in Figures 3–10 and 3–11) and the Lancelot (shown in Figures 3–12 and 3–13) can be adapted for ice carving, though they were originally designed for hobbyists, woodcarvers, and model makers. Both open new dimensions with their ability to straight cut, undercut, carve, sculpt, hollow, and gouge in any direction, removing large amounts of ice rapidly. They allow excellent control with little effort, resulting in rapid ice removal and shaping in confined as well as large areas. Not only will they increase productivity and creativity, but they also may replace other tools.

Lancelot is a 4-inch diameter 22-tooth saw, chain mounted between two discs. It fits most 4-inch or 4½-inch disc/angle grinders. Percival is a 2-inch diameter, 8-tooth, saw chain ice carving accessory that fits mini die grinders and flexible shaft machines with ¼-inch collets or chucks. Percival is available in two shaft lengths: 4-inch and 6-inch, both with handgrip safety guard. The 4-inch model provides excellent control for close work, while the 6-inch unit allows for extended-reach waste removal in hard-to-reach places. It is also used for undercutting an ice carving.

These unique tools allow for rapid ice shaping and removal for any size project. Both products can easily be sharpened with a ⁵⁄₃₂-inch chain saw file, and replacement chain is available. Both tools are available from King Arthur's Tools, see list of associations and manufacturers.

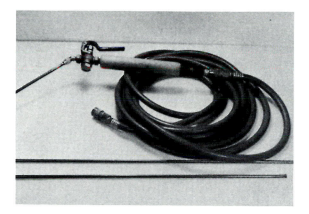

FIGURE 3–9 **Steam Hose** and **Steam Gun** Used for carving ice with steam. Steam hose, steam valve, and copper tubing shown above.

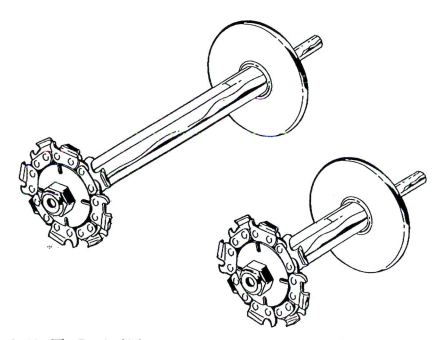

FIGURE 3–10 **The Percival** This ice-carving saw is available in two shaft lengths: 4-inch and 6-inch.

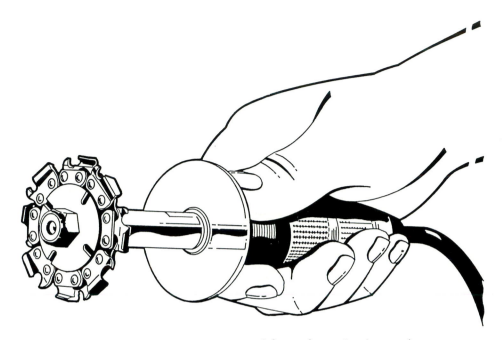

FIGURE 3–11   The Percival is a convenient tool for undercutting ice carvings.

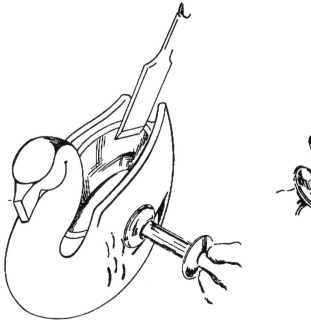

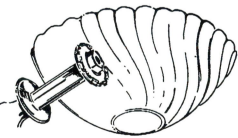

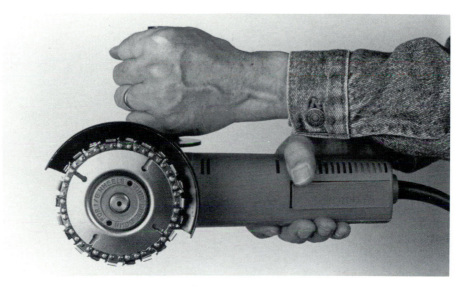

FIGURE 3–12 **The Lancelot** This saw is excellent for removing small pieces from ice blocks.

FIGURE 3–13 Various styles of cutting heads make the Lancelot versatile and useful.

Chapter 4

Types of Ice

$\mathcal{I}$ce blocks vary in quality and sizes depending on the region of the country. I shall attempt to give the beginner some information on the variety of ice blocks available.

The ice block that is most widely available in the United States weighs 300 pounds, measures 10 by 20 inches at its base, and stands 40–42 inches high, as shown in Figure 4–1. A *feather,* or core, runs from the top about two-thirds the length of the block. This takes away from the clarity of the ice, but is not much of a disadvantage in carving.

The ice block shown in Figure 4–2 is approximately one-third taller than the block described above, and is manufactured in the same manner. It is not as easily obtainable; however, you may be able to find it in larger cities.

Ice manufactured in large manufacturing plants typically has a cloudy core because of the way it is made. Water is frozen in molds while air is bubbled through the water. This air comes through tubes inserted at the top of the mold. As the outside of the mold is the coldest, the bubbling helps equalize the water temperature throughout the mold; it also helps extract impurities that would cloud the ice. Shortly before the ice is completely frozen, the tubes are removed, leaving an empty core. This is filled and frozen to complete the block. This core freezes cloudy because it does not receive the benefit of the air agitation. Some of the steps in this traditional ice-manufacturing process are shown in Figures 4–6 through 4–8.

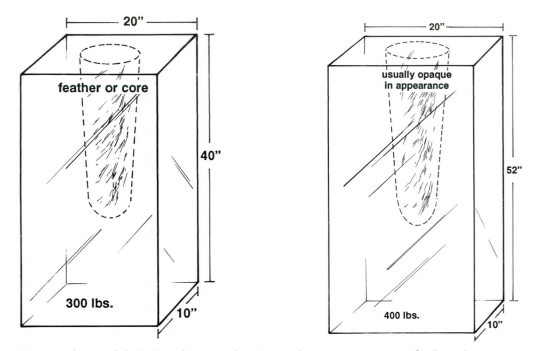

FIGURES 4–1 and 4–2 Ice plants produce ice with an opaque core or feather; the opaque core is created during the final stages of freezing.

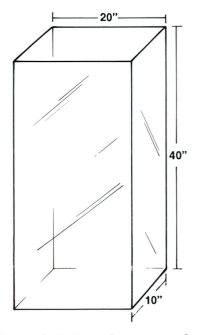

FIGURE 4–3 Ice with no core or feather can be manufactured in 300-pound blocks.

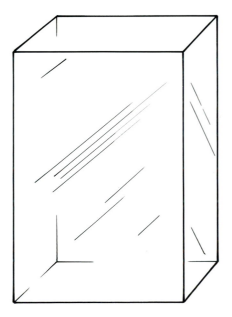

FIGURE 4–4 Clear ice can also be harvested from lakes. Lake ice weights vary from hundreds of pounds to tons.

The block shown in Figure 4–3 is the most desired and recommended type of ice. It does not have the opaque center core typical of ice manufactured in ice plants and is cheaper and superior to lake ice.

Although ice of this clarity could be a product of ice harvesting from lakes, clear blocks of this manageable size are more likely produced by special ice-manufacturing machines. The equipment for manufacturing this clear, core-free ice requires minimal space and is reasonably priced for hotels and professionals. Clinebell's Equipment Company makes a unit that will produce two 300-pound blocks of clear, transparent ice in approximately 36 hours. See Figure 4–5. To contact Clinebell's Equipment Company, see list of associations and manufacturers.

FIGURE 4–5 An ice-manufacturing machine made by Clinebell's Equipment Company, Inc.

FIGURE 4–6 In traditional ice-manufacturing plants, air under pressure keeps water circulating while it freezes.

This ice is more expensive to buy than ice from large ice-manufacturing plants, but it is still cheaper and more readily available than ice harvested from lakes.

Clear, natural ice, as shown in Figure 4–4, can be harvested from lakes in Alaska and other colder regions of the United States. It can be cut and harvested in any size from a few hundred pounds to several tons and moved with fork lifts. Because of the expense and difficulty of harvesting lake ice, it is generally used only for major ice sculpturing competitions.

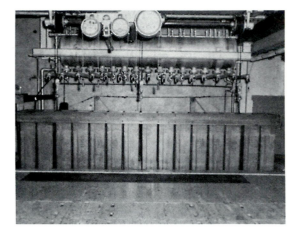

FIGURE 4–7 Temperatures are rigidly controlled in ice-manufacturing plants.

FIGURE 4–8 Finished ice blocks are "poured" out of molds and ready for storage or delivery.

Stacking Ice Blocks for Large Carvings

For carvings needing multiple ice blocks, ice blocks can be cut or split and stacked in various positions, according to the planned carving. If you are planning to leave the blocks in temperatures above freezing, the combination of the pressure from weight of the ice and the melting will bond the ice blocks together, as long as they are flat. If the ice blocks are stored in a freezer, you can bond them with salt or aerosol sprays designed to remove gum and tar. For some reason, these sprays offer an effective bond for ice pieces.

See Figure 4–9 for suggested stacking methods.

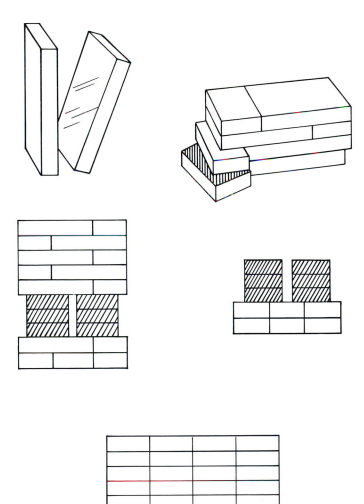

FIGURE 4–9   Stacking techniques for bonding ice blocks together for larger sculptures.

Chapter 5

Styrofoam Carvings

Styrofoam—for Long-Lasting Carvings

When you want carvings that look like snow but do not melt . . . carvings that can be used again and again . . . make them of out Styrofoam. Amateurs should consider it a good medium for practicing their technique.

It is easy to sculpt Styrofoam using the same tools and basic techniques as for ice carvings. It is lightweight, easily worked, and does not chip readily. And, since Styrofoam is so inexpensive, you can put a lot of imagination into your creations with amusing and interesting results.

Styrofoam is easily available in blocks measuring approximately 12 by 36 inches and in thicknesses of one, two, and four inches. It is obtainable in several other sizes. Ask your vendor about the variety of Styrofoam sizes offered.

Its maker, the Dow Chemical Company of Midland, Michigan, describes Styrofoam as "expanded polystyrene." Several blocks of it may be bonded together to make a larger unit for carving big figures. Styrofoam and ethafoam (a similar material) may also be bonded to metal, wood, masonry, cloth, paper, glass, and plastics. It may be used indoors or outdoors.

The surface of Styrofoam may be coated to protect it from soiling, weathering, and other damage, or simply to decorate it for your display. Coatings may also be used to make it fire-resistant.

To carve Styrofoam, begin with a template, as you would for an ice carving, and scribe out the silhouette of the carving chosen. For larger or complicated figures it's best to start with smaller units, cut them individually, then assemble them. If the block of foam is too big, it becomes difficult to cut.

First, assemble the pieces in a block and transfer the design from your paper template.

Lay out the pieces separately and cut them with a jigsaw or hand coping saw.

Join the pieces together with special Styrofoam glue. Follow the gluing instructions carefully; Styrofoam glue has special characteristics.

Let the assembled figure dry for a day or two before working it further.

Detail the assembled carving with a sharp knife or any sharp electrical tool.

You also can use the "hot-wire" method of cutting Styrofoam in which low-voltage current is run through a nickel-chromium resistance wire to cause it to heat. The wire slices neatly through the foam.

The best way to smooth the surface of styrofoam is to rub it with another piece of Styrofoam; use a scrap to shape and smooth the surface of your carving.

The finishing touches depend upon your own creative sense. Small scraps of colored felt are very effective trimmings. For example, the reindeer shown in Figure 5–2 has eyes of blue felt circles and a nose of red felt. The snowman has small black circles for eyes and large red felt circles for buttons.

Ribbon is also useful for decoration and may be obtained in a variety of beautiful colors and textures, including many that are waterproof and may be used outdoors.

For a special effect, Styrofoam also can be coated with chocolate or tallow.

There are endless possibilities for displays using Styrofoam. Here are a few examples:

Baskets, vases: May be filled with winter bouquets or realistic artificial flowers.

Cornucopias (horns of plenty): May be shown with artificial fruits or coins pouring out.

Reindeer: Reindeer drawing a sleigh full of gaily wrapped gift packages will create a festive atmosphere. Ribbons may be used as reins.

Department stores: Displays for windows, ledges, and counters.

Florists: Vases or baskets can be used in windows or for interior displays with flowers that will not wilt or fade.

Holiday decorations: For all sorts of businesses.

Stage props: For amateur or professional productions.

Parties or special functions: In hotels and restaurants, where more perishable ice carvings would not be practical. For instance, smaller restaurants that cannot afford ice carvings can, in time, assemble a collection of Styrofoam sculptures for all sorts of occasions.

Children's parties: Offer particularly good opportunities for the skillful carver. Imagine the delight of the small host or hostess who may keep the most important part of the party trimmings!

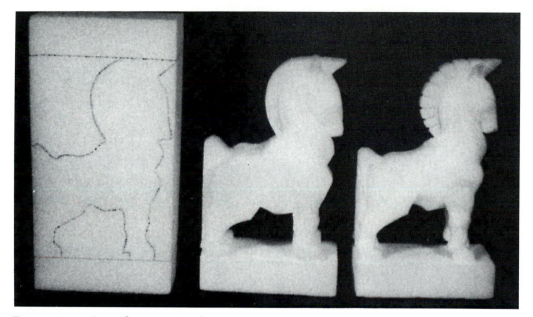

FIGURE 5–1 Steps for carving a figure out of Styrofoam.

FIGURE 5–2 A finished Styrofoam figure.

FIGURES 5–3, 5–4, and 5–5 Sculptures carved from Styrofoam.

Chapter 6

Starting to Carve

The Basic Shapes

If you have never done an ice carving, start with something simple that you can use, such as baskets, punchbowls or lettering.

Artists say that every object you can think of—from a vase to a tree or house or animal or human form—begins with one of four basic shapes, as shown in Figures 6–1 through 6–4. Complicated carvings are made of combinations of two or more basic shapes.

The cube may be used for carving a box, boat, house, castle, relish tray, or as a base for most large carvings.

The cone shown in Figure 6–2 may be shaped into a tree, a vase, the spout of Aladdin's lamp, a candle flame, the body or tail of a fish or an animal.

The cylinder, Figure 6–3, may form a candle, numerals, letters, smoke stacks for ships, and so forth.

The sphere, Figure 6–4, is the basis for bowls, vases, and the heads of people or animals.

The simplest display piece you can make is a logo encased in an ice block. Merely saw the ice block in half (lengthwise if it's rectangular). Protect the insignia you want to display by wrapping it in clear plastic. Put this between the two halves of the ice block and freeze them together with the insignia inside. You can bond the

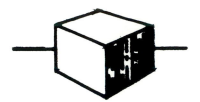

FIGURE 6–1 **Cube.**

FIGURE 6–2 **Cone.**

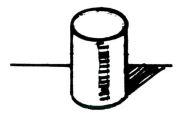

FIGURE 6–3 **Cylinder.**

FIGURE 6–4 **Sphere** or **ball.**

two blocks of ice with some water and salt; salt will lower the temperature of the water and hasten freezing. Compounds in spray cleaners suitable for removing gum can also help the ice to bond.

Illuminate the finished sculpture from the back, and you have a dramatic show piece with very little effort. This is suitable for featuring the insignia of a club, school, college, business or fraternal organization, the burgee of a yacht club, a silhouette of a famous person (as for a national holiday), a check or currency to dramatize a prize in a contest.

Once you have chosen the subject of your carving, scribe the outline of a drawing using a sharp tool, or use a template as described in Chapter 9.

Planning to Carve

Planning is important when it comes to ice carving. The ice should be placed on a movable wooden stand about two feet high. Your tools should be placed on a bench or table so they are not underfoot. Check all power cords to ensure that they are waterproof and are not cracked or frayed. It is essential to make sure that all electrical tools are U.L. approved, and that outlet connections are waterproof. Waterproof electrical connections are critical and could protect you from dangerous or fatal electrical accidents.

The floor should have a drainage system. If it does not, make sure a floor squeegee is available to move ice chips and water away from the working area.

Clothing should be comfortable and waterproof. To protect your hands, wear waterproof gloves; to protect your feet, wear safety-toe waterproof shoes. Wear goggles to shield your eyes from flying ice chips, and ear plugs to soften the noise of the chain saw. See Figure 6–5.

For easier carving or cutting, first lay your block of ice on a piece of Styrofoam larger than the base of your ice block. This elevates the ice and also protects the blade of your saw and the sharp edge of your tools from the table. See Figure 6–6.

When you finish carving, it is essential that the tools be dried, chisels sharpened, and everything put away in its proper place.

FIGURE 6–5   Make sure you have taken the proper safety precautions before beginning your carving.

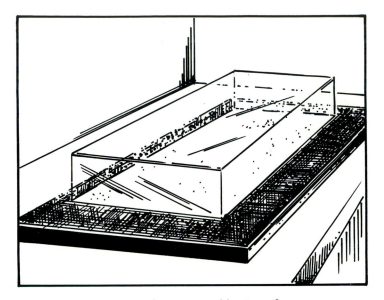

FIGURE 6–6   Ice properly supported by Styrofoam.

Conditions

Carvings can be done outdoors at moderate temperatures or in walk-in institutional-size refrigerators. A walk-in box or institutional refrigerator is generally between 36° and 42°F. Avoid carving in direct sunlight or windy areas, as these conditions will cause the ice to melt too fast.

When you plan an ice carving, carefully consider the size of ice you will be carving. Make sure you allow time to properly condition the ice. This process is called tempering and involves bringing the ice to the proper temperature for carving. To temper ice, leave it out of the freezer for several hours. Ice that has just been removed from the freezer will be too hard and brittle to carve.

Chapter 7

Setting Up Your Carvings

Setting Up Your Display

Try decorating your carving with greenery. An ice basket may be filled with fresh flowers or with a winter bouquet. Many pieces can be surrounded with ferns or flowers. You could also tie colored ribbons, bows, or other accessories to your sculpture.

An important thing to remember when setting up a carving is drainage. Your carving should sit on wooden blocks that are placed in a pan large enough to hold the water that will collect from the melting ice; or in a pan with a petcock and hose that allow the water to drain off into a hidden container.

The pan can be surrounded by aluminum foil, a table cloth, Styrofoam, ferns, flowers, ribbons, or colored cellophane to disguise it.

It is most important that the table holding the carving be strong and sturdy. It should, of course, be checked well ahead of time.

Ice formed into punchbowls, shrimp boats, and relish trays is excellent for keeping edibles and liquids cold; if they are used for an outdoor buffet, they also help keep away insects.

Winter carvings displayed outdoors are crowd pleasers, especially for Winter Carnivals.

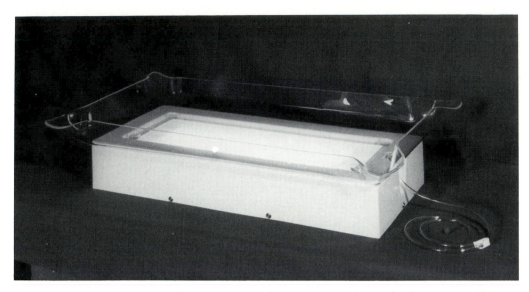

FIGURE 7–1 An ice carving display tray may be used to display and enhance your ice carving. You could try to underlight it for better effect. A draining hose should be supplied with the tray.

Lighting Your Display

Lighting plays a very important part in an ice carving display. A light with a revolving color wheel placed at the back will give a steady show of colored light through the ice. A carving standing alone may be spotlighted by one bright white or colored light to make it the highlight of a larger display, as on a buffet table.

Some ice carvers prefer to place colored electric lights under their carvings, directly inside the pan. I do not recommend this method, however, because water from the melting ice might drip on the wiring and short-circuit the party.

When using spotlights, be sure the source of light is far enough from the ice carving so that its heat will not hasten melting.

Finishing Touches

Carvers use different methods for smoothing the surface of a carving. You may, for instance, pour water over your carving and then rub hot towels over it to make it glisten.

The simplest and best method, however, is to allow the carving to stand at room temperature for an hour before its debut. Just enough of the surface melts to make the carving gleam and glisten.

Importance of the Base

Every carving should have a base. It should be at least the full size of the ice block's bottom and four to five inches high. For decorative purposes, it is generally more desirable to have an oversized base on small carvings. A large base makes a small carving a special point of interest. Table decorations can conceal the base to further enhance the display. And, the base can be scored in a diamond shape or other design to capture prism reflections and refractions of light rays for dramatic sparkle.

Some good examples showing ice carving bases are in photos in Figures 10–33, 10–35, 10–37, 10–39, 10–41 and 10–43.

FIGURE 7–2 Mounting your carving on an ice base can enhance the presentation. The swan shown here was created from a mold. The base was incorporated into the mold's design.

Chapter 8

Special Circumstances

Transporting or Moving Ice Carvings

Ice carvings are more fragile and brittle than glass, and must be handled with extreme care. Any sudden shock or jarring may cause the piece to break.

Large carvings should be set up in advance of the party on a substantial table that will not be jostled as guests enter or leave the room.

Smaller carvings may be carried in on trays held aloft by waiters as the dramatic high point of the party. Room lights may be dimmed and carvings illuminated by flashlights set in openings underneath.

Repairing Breaks or Welding

When creating a large sculpture, it sometimes makes sense to carve appendages from separate ice pieces and attach them. Bonding these pieces together is called welding. Welding is especially helpful for assembling sculptures having long tails, necks, or other appendages. If your ice is not ideally shaped for your subject, welding allows you the flexibility to carve your sculpture in pieces and weld them together. To make a stronger bond between ice pieces, you may also want to notch the area to be joined on the main part of the sculpture and carve an extension on the end of the appendage to fit the notch (see Figure 10–19).

If you know the tricks of bonding ice to ice you can also fix breaks successfully. Welding or mending breaks both involve the same basic bonding chemistry.

You can bond your ice pieces together with the following techniques:

1. If the carving is in a warm place, sprinkle salt liberally over both surfaces of the break. Replace the broken piece and apply pressure by holding the joint together for two or three minutes. Pour water over the carving and allow it to stand for a while.

2. Should the break be serious, as the neck or wingtips of a swan or bird, hold the broken piece in place and pack wet snow around the cracked area, building it up a bit. Apply pressure and allow it to stand for a while; then scrape off excess ice or snow. The snow must be free from crystals and very fine. Real snow, ice shavings from a chain saw or chisel, or shavings from an ice plant are most suitable.

3. Dry ice may be held against the broken joint for a few moments until the meltage freezes. Never handle dry ice with your bare hands; contact with it will cause severe burns. Wear heavy waterproof gloves or pick it up with a folded towel.

4. Spraying liquid CO_2 on the break and holding the appendage parts together for a minute or so will also create a strong bond.

5. Chewing gum and candle wax remover from an aerosol can is commonly used for breaks and for attaching appendages. Spray liberally at the joint and hold for a minute or so. Read the label to make sure the product is ozone friendly.

If a piece broken from the carving is too small to carve a replacement, the missing piece can be formed on the carving by building it up with wet snow. The piece replaced will last longer if the carving is set in the freezer until firm.

Chapter 9

Design Patterns

Design Patterns

A template is a cardboard cutout that you can place against the ice block and use as a guide in scribing the silhouette of the design.

Use graph paper to transpose the drawings in this book onto cardboard. For a full-size carving, each square in the scale drawings in this book equals one inch on your final graph. For a half-size carving, each square equals half an inch on your graph or template. The graph paper will allow you easily to increase or reduce the size of your figure, depending on your needs.

The method of making your template is:

1. Draw a graph of four-inch squares for a full-scale carving (or two-inch squares for half-size) on cardboard.

2. Place graph paper on the scale drawing in the text. This should be transparent enough that you can see the drawing through it.

3. Plot on the large squares a series of points that correspond to the points at which the outline of the scale drawings intersect the lines on the paper.

4. Connect the points with a solid line.

Tracing

Select your design from this book, a photograph, or another source. Use tissue paper or tracing paper to trace the outline. Transfer this pattern through carbon paper onto graph paper. Then project, as above, to get the size you want. Cut out the cardboard pattern to use as a template in scribing the ice.

Models

By using a small model of the work to be shaped in ice, the carver can gain a better sense of proportion and overall conception of the design. Small, inexpensive plastic or wooden models of animals, boats, autos, and so forth, may be found in many stores. These are of great help. A somewhat more involved method is to carve a miniature figure from a bar of soap first and use it as a model when working with ice.

Molds for Ice Carving

Molds for ice carving are available in many shapes, sizes, and subjects. They are made from latex, rubber, and plastic. Mold costs vary according to the mold size and shape. Available sizes range from six inches to full sizes of two to three feet in height. Unless you use a large volume of carvings the investment in molds is unwarranted.

These molds are available through hotel and equipment suppliers and come with detailed instructions depending on the figure.

Creative Ice Bowls

The punch bowls pictured are examples of the creative touch that is added when objects are frozen into place inside ice sculptures. With technology made possible by machines such as the Creative Ice Bowl Machine®, carvers can freeze flowers and other decorative items into the ice. This process personalizes ice pieces both in color and concept.

The decoration on the inside is the starting point for these sculptures. Carve the exterior to a shape that complements the decorative elements inside. For example, freeze roses inside and carve the outside in the shape of a heart for romantic presentations. Spiral a vine throughout the bowl and carve the outside with leaf patterns for a garden party or luncheon. The punch bowl shape allows the sculpture to be useful, keeping shrimp, cheese, cold soups, vegetables and fruits fresh and cold.

FIGURE 9–1 Punch bowl molded in a lattice design.

FIGURE 9–2 Punch bowl molded with a designed edge.

Special accessories allow the carver to produce cylinders and blocks for use as pedestals and vases or in multiple block arrangements. Carved vases can be used as table centerpieces, or can be used to display bottles of wine or liquor. The molds are available from Creative Ice/Ice Rentals, Inc., see list of associations and manufacturers.

FIGURE 9–3 Elaborate punch bowl with flowers frozen into the base.

FIGURE 9–4 Punch bowl with flowers frozen into the ice.

FIGURE 9–5 Machinery available for creating unusual ice creations.

Chapter **10**
. . . .

Specific Projects

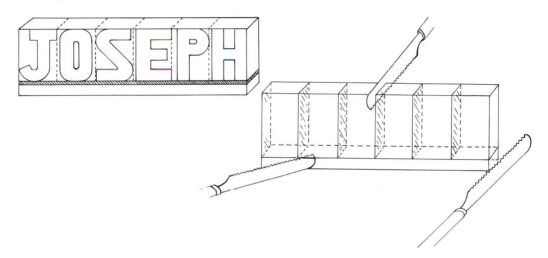

FIGURE 10–1 **Letters** Plan for a template and steps for carving.

Letters

1. Plot the letters to be carved onto graph paper keeping in mind the size and proportions of each figure.

2. As shown in the following illustration, plan and separate each letter; this will make them easier to carve.

3. Remove approximately two to three inches from both front and back of the ice form to narrow the block. How much you cut away depends, of course, on how long the carving must last.

4. Shape each letter with your chisel.

Numerals

1. Make your template as in the illustration and scribe it onto the ice block.

2. With your saw, separate the numerals as shown by the dotted lines in the illustration. Remove the excess ice.

3. Silhouette the numerals with your ice chipper or chisel and finish shaping the figure.

4. Define the wreath with your finishing tools. This detail will add sparkle if you backlight or spotlight the sculpture.

FIGURE 10–2 *Photo and carving provided by Steve Rose.*

FIGURE 10–3 Numerals Plan for a template and steps for carving.

FIGURE 10–4　*Photo and carving provided by Steve Rose.*

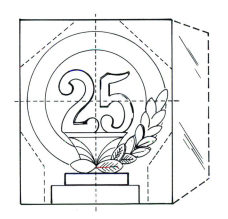

FIGURE 10–5　**Numerals Surrounded by a Wreath** Plan for a template.

Silhouettes

Silhouette carvings are very simple, attractive display pieces. Novelty stores sell large cardboard illustrations of Lincoln, Washington, Santa, Cupid, and many others. Silhouettes can be made of any color heavy construction paper or thin plastic material.

1. Make a template of the desired shape, (heart, star, shield, etc.) and scribe it onto the ice block.

2. Using a large saw, remove the pieces of ice not covered by the pattern.

3. Chip away excess ice surrounding the desired shape. With a large saw, cut through the center core of the ice block. (See dotted line in Figure 10–6.)

4. Slide the silhouette into this opening. Seal the cut with wet snow.

5. Dramatic lighting with background lights will make these display pieces extremely effective.

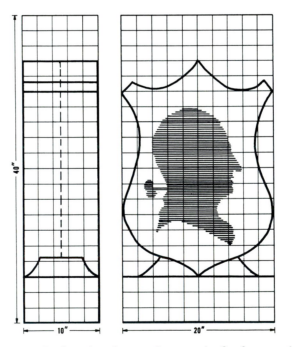

FIGURE 10–6 Silhouette Reduced-scale template graphs for front and side.

Logos

1. Prepare the design of your logo full-size on a piece of transparent paper. This will become your template.

2. Lay the ice on a piece of Styrofoam for easier work (see Figure 10–7).

3. Use a sander to smooth off the surface of the ice on both sides.

4. Place your template on top of the ice in reverse, as shown below. This is the back of Figure—the logo will appear in the correct direction when displayed.

5. Use a steam iron to smooth out the front surface, as well as to get the logo pattern or design to stick to the back of the ice. The ironed paper will freeze to the ice.

6. Using a die grinder and following the paper pattern, cut the logo into the back surface, through the paper.

7. Pack the cavity of your design with snow. The white areas will contrast with the smooth, clear ice and give your logo greater definition. (If no snow is available, use the snow created when you cut the ice with the chain saw.)

FIGURE 10–7 Logo Steps for carving.

Hummingbirds and Flowers

1. Prepare your graph or stencil on transparent paper by following the illustrations provided. It must be full-size.

2. Iron the template to the back of ice.

3. Lay the ice on a piece of Styrofoam for easier work.

4. Cut the outline of the ice shape as illustrated and remove all excess ice.

5. Once you have the basic shape cut, turn the ice front-side-down onto the foam. Place the silhouette of birds and flowers onto the ice. Follow the instructions in Figure 10–7 for detailed instructions. (See previous page.)

6. As with the logo sculpture, pack snow into the chiseled cavity to give contrast to your design.

7. Finish the base as illustrated.

FIGURE 10–8 **Hummingbirds and Flowers** Plan for a carving template.

Ship in a Bottle

1. Prepare your graph or stencil by following the illustrations provided, or use a model if available.

2. Iron the template to the back of the ice.

3. Lay the ice on a piece of Styrofoam for easier work.

4. Remove with a saw any ice not required. Please refer to page 55 for detailed instructions.

5. Shape out the shape of the bottle with chisels and use a die grinder for detail.

6. Turn the ice over so that the front side of the bottle is toward the foam. Place on the ice the silhouette of a ship to be etched onto the bottle. With a die grinder, etch out the ship's design.

7. To add contrast, pack snow into the cavity created by the design.

8. Create a base to show off your carving.

FIGURE 10–9 Ship in a Bottle Plan for a carving template.

Bowls and Dishes

Bowls and dishes are good carvings for beginners, and are very useful for holding cold foods and liquids at buffets and receptions.

Any shape, size, or design can be made. The step-by-step drawings shown in Figures 10–10 through 10–14 will give you some ideas, or you may use your own style and design.

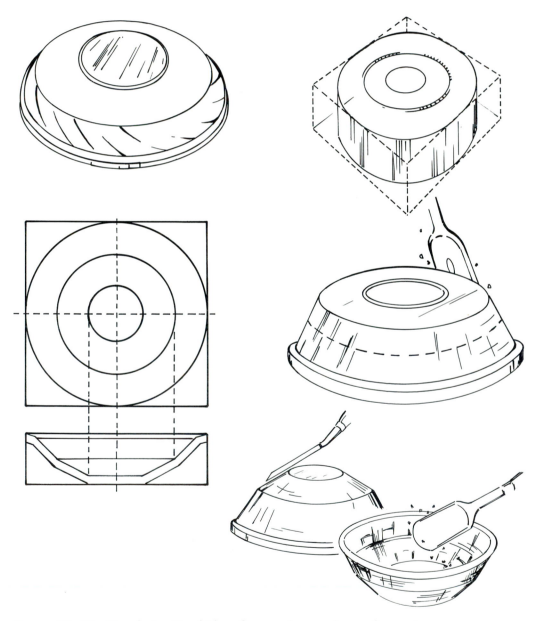

FIGURE 10–10 Simple Ice Bowl Plans for templates and steps for carving.

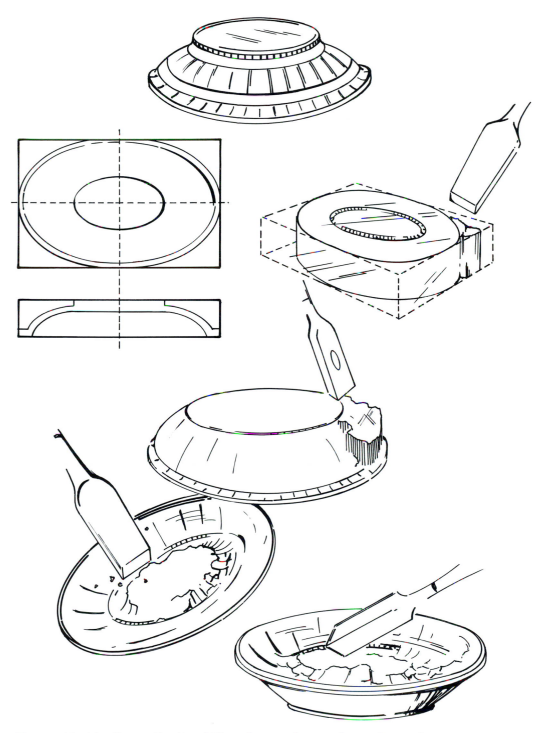

FIGURE 10–11 Ornate Ice Bowl Plans for templates and steps for carving.

Bowl and Dishes
Various Shapes & Designs

1. Lay the piece of ice down on a piece of Styrofoam. You may set your bowl on a base like the one shown in Figure 10–11.

2. Prepare your paper template using the designs shown in Figures 10–10 through 10–14.

3. Scribe the pattern onto the ice.

4. Shape the ice by removing the excess from the outside edge of your chosen design.

5. Using your tools as shown in the following illustration, form and highlight carving.

FIGURE 10–12 Fluted Ice Bowl Plans for templates and steps for carving.

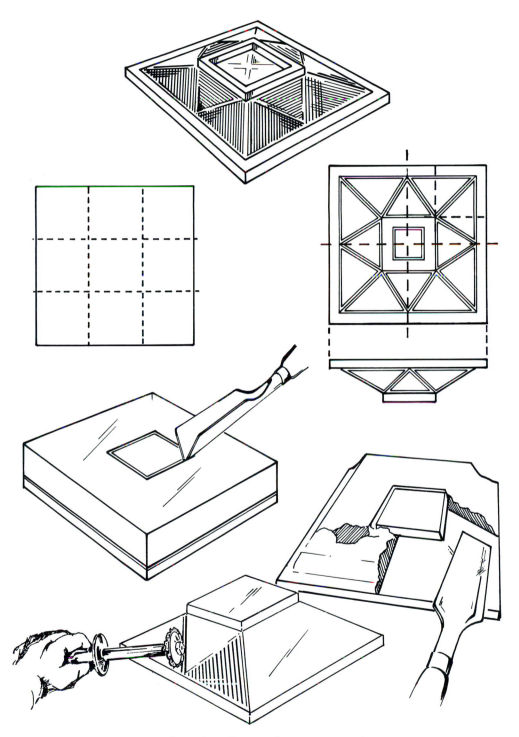

FIGURE 10–13 Square Ice Plate Plans for templates and steps for carving.

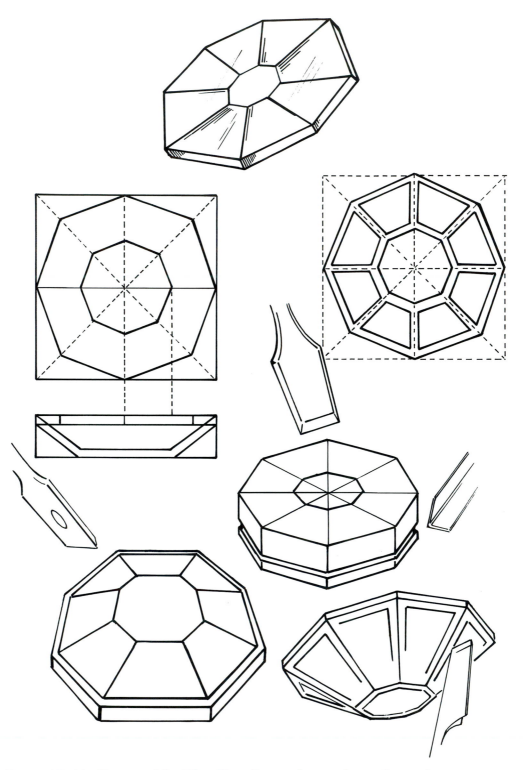

FIGURE 10–14   Octagonal Ice Plate Plans for templates and steps for carving.

Flower Vase

1. Make a flower-vase template on graph paper from the drawing shown in Figure 10–15. Scribe pattern onto the ice block.

2. With a large saw, remove the larger pieces of ice not covered by the pattern outline.

3. Chip away excess ice with the shaver, leaving an evenly balanced shape.

4. With your ice chipper, dig an eight-to-ten-inch well at the top to hold flowers.

5. With a die grinder, form a design on the outside of the vase, as shown in Figure 10–15.

With this illustration 10–15, even a beginner could carve a great vase.

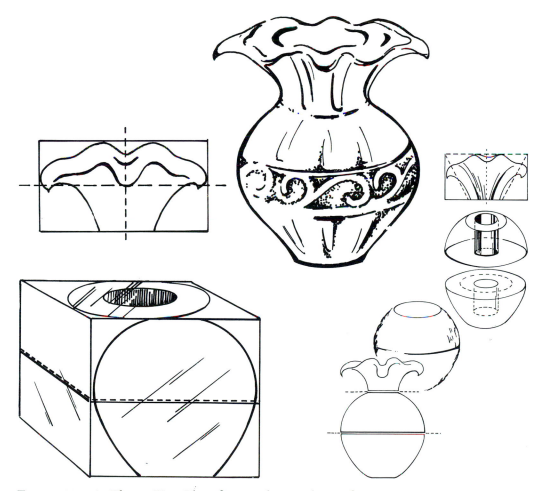

FIGURE 10–15   Flower Vase Plans for templates and steps for carving.

Duck

1. Prepare your graph or stencil by following the illustrations provided. Use a model if available.

2. Lay the ice on a piece of Styrofoam for easier work.

3. Remove any ice not required with a saw.

4. Shape the duck's head with chisels, using a die grinder for detail.

5. Shape out the tail as shown in the illustration.

6. Smooth out and detail, accentuating the subject with a die grinder.

7. Using your chisel, hollow out a bowl on the back of the duck to hold food or flowers.

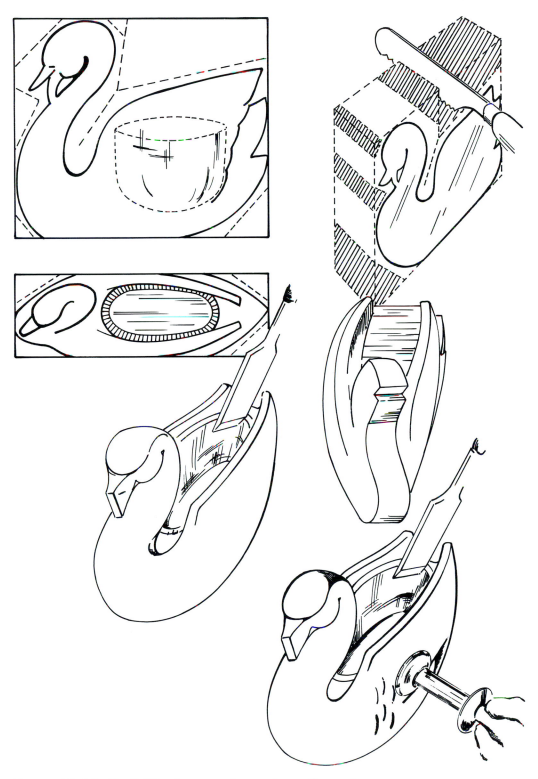

FIGURE 10–16 Duck Plan for a template and steps for carving.

Tiger

1. Prepare your graph or stencil by following the illustrations provided. Use a model if available.

2. Lay the ice on a piece of Styrofoam for easier work.

3. Remove with a saw any ice not required.

4. Shape out face and ears with chisels, using a die grinder for detail.

5. Shape out tail and legs as shown in the illustration.

6. Smooth out and detail, accentuating the subject with a die grinder.

7. Place the portion of tail with peg end into the notch of the body using wet snow to hold them together. See illustration.

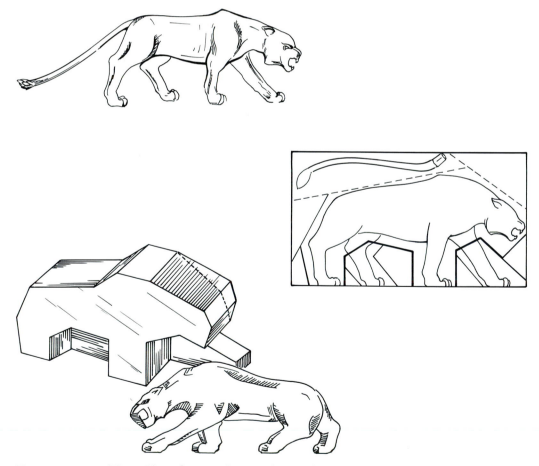

FIGURE 10–17 Tiger Plans for templates and steps for carving.

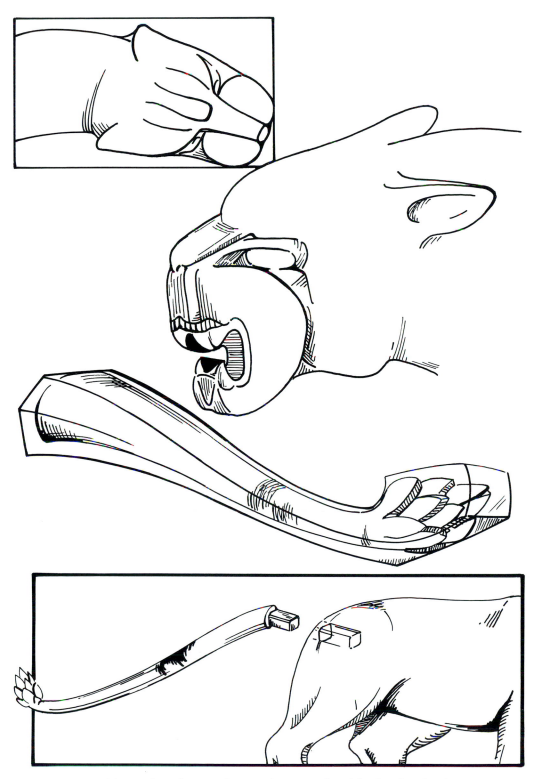

FIGURE 10–18 Tiger Plans for templates and carving detail for head and tail.

Eagle

1. Prepare your graph or stencil by following the illustrations provided. Use a model if available. Although complicated, this piece is carved from one block of ice.

2. Lay the ice on a piece of Styrofoam for easier work.

3. Remove with a saw any ice not required.

4. Shape out the eagle's head and beak with chisels, using a die grinder for the detail of the wings and feathers.

5. Shape out tail, legs, and talons as shown in the illustration.

6. Smooth out and detail, accentuating the subject with a die grinder.

7. Finish the base according to subject as illustrated.

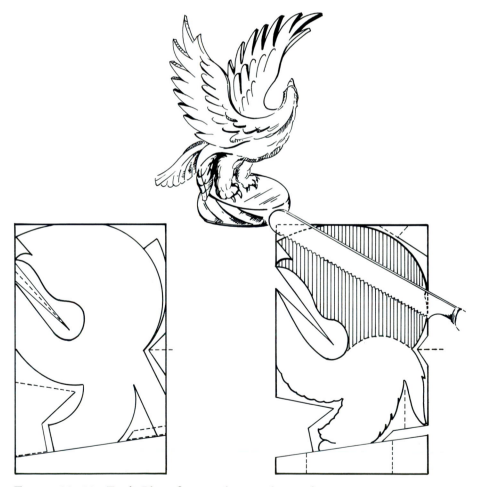

FIGURE 10–19 Eagle Plans for templates and steps for carving.

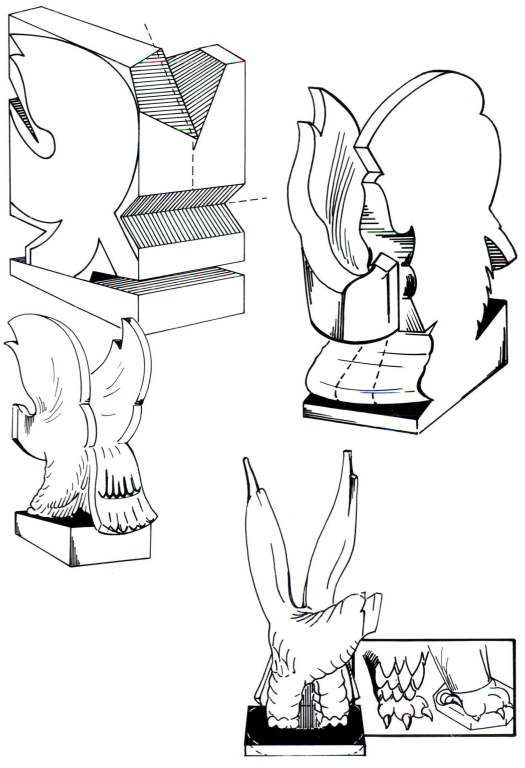

FIGURE 10–20   Eagle Steps for carving, continued.

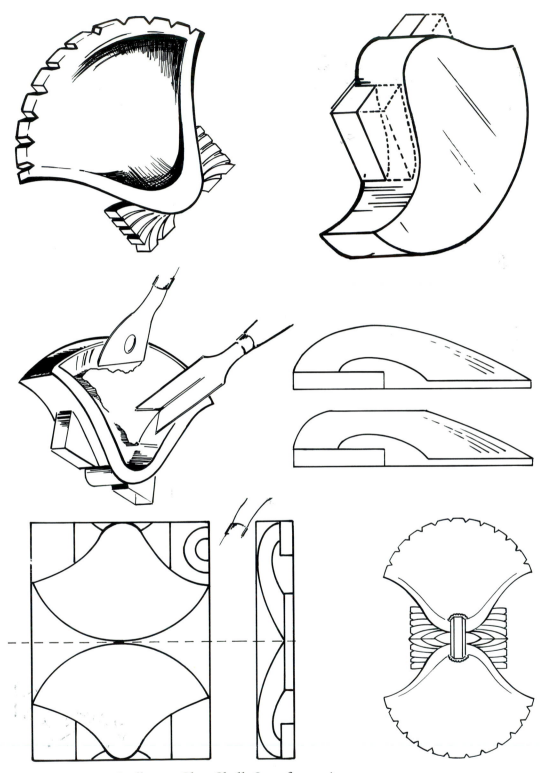

FIGURE 10–21   **Scallop or Clam Shells** Steps for carving.

Scallop or Clam Shells

1. Study the illustration before starting.

2. Split a full block of ice into two even portions.

3. Lay the ice pieces on some Styrofoam and scribe the shell designs onto the ice, as in Figure 10–21.

4. Saw off all excess ice from the outside of the shell. Save the end cuts and incorporate them into the finished carving, as shown in the illustration.

5. Using chisels, hollow out the inside portion of the shell.

6. Assemble the shell and contour the outer surface of the shell.

7. To finish the shell, detail the outside. Grooves will give the effect of a scallop.

8. Half shells can be carved for serving seafood products.

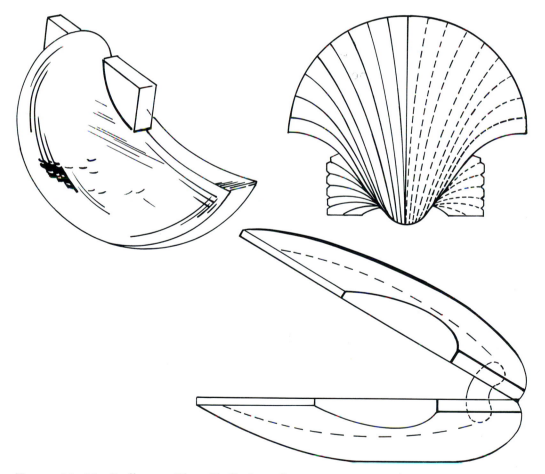

FIGURE 10–22 Scallop or Clam Shells Steps for carving, continued.

Standing Rabbit

1. Using a graph to make your template, scribe the pattern onto the face of the ice block.

2. Chip away all excess ice with a shaver, leaving a silhouette.

3. With a saw, split the ice between the rabbit's ears.

4. Shape out the ears and round off the face and body of the rabbit.

5. After shaping, groove holes for the eyes with a ½-inch chisel. Bore holes at the sides of the mouth to affix pipe cleaners for the rabbit's whiskers.

6. To hold the pipe cleaners in place, pack a little wet snow around them.

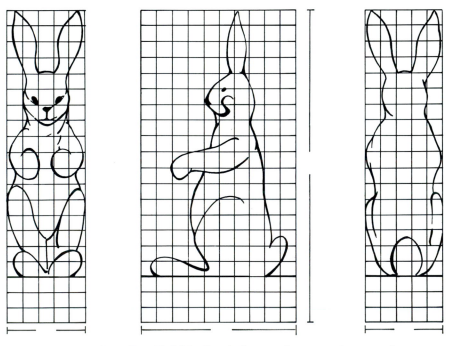

FIGURE 10–23 **Standing Rabbit** Graph for creating a carving template.

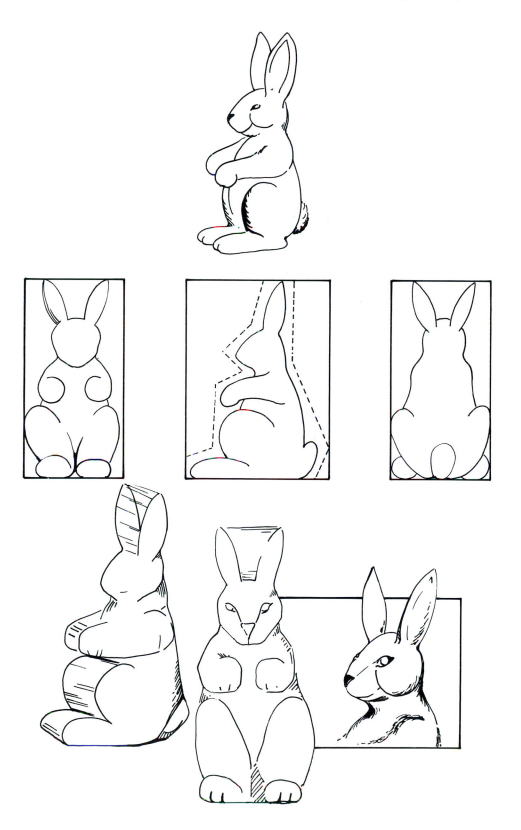

Running Rabbit

1. Prepare your graph or stencil by following the illustrations provided. Use a model if available.

2. Lay the ice on a piece of Styrofoam for easier work.

3. With a saw, remove any ice not required. Keep in mind the two outlined triangles of ice will be incorporated into the finished carving.

4. Shape out the face and ears with chisels and use a die grinder for detail.

5. Shape out the tail per illustration.

6. Smooth out and detail, accentuating the subject with a die grinder.

7. Use the two triangular pieces of ice to form base for carving.

8. Finish the base as illustrated.

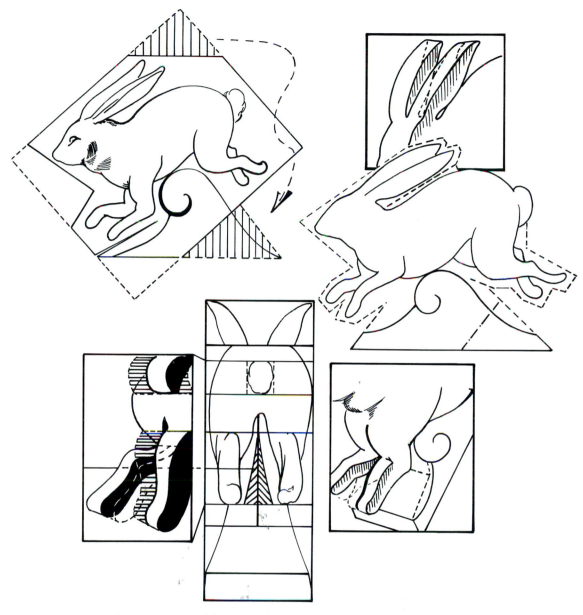

FIGURE 10–24 Running Rabbit Plans for templates and steps for carving.

Dog

1. Prepare your graph or stencil by following the illustrations provided. Use a model if available.

2. Lay the ice on a piece of Styrofoam for easier work.

3. With a saw, remove any ice not required for subject.

4. Shape the dog's face and ears with chisels, using a die grinder for detail.

5. Shape out the tail and legs per illustration.

6. Smooth out and detail, accentuating the subject with a die grinder.

7. Create a base of your choice.

FIGURE 10–25 Dog Plans for templates and steps for carving.

Brown Bear

1. Prepare your graph or stencil by following the illustrations provided. Use a model if available.

2. Lay the ice on a piece of Styrofoam for easier work.

3. With a saw, remove any ice not required.

4. Shape out the face and ears with chisels and use a die grinder for detail.

5. Shape out tail and legs as shown on the illustration.

6. Smooth out and detail, accentuating the subject with a die grinder.

7. Create a base with another ice block.

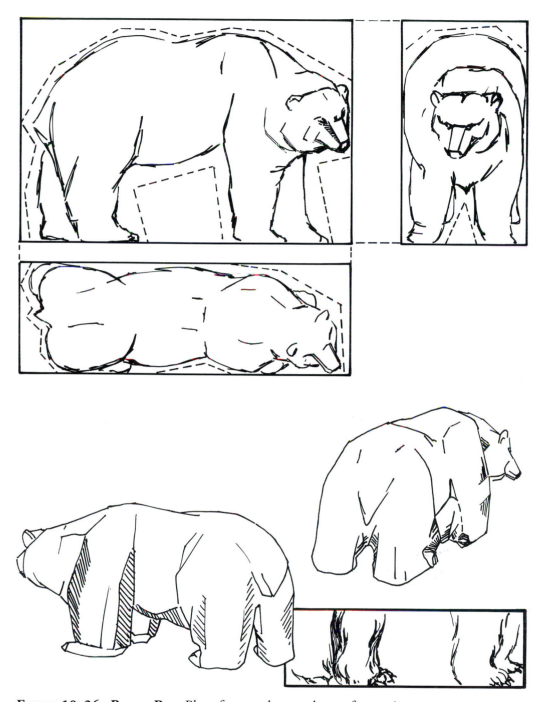

FIGURE 10–26 **Brown Bear** Plans for templates and steps for carving.

Squirrel

1. Prepare your graph or stencil by following the illustrations provided. Use a model if available.

2. Lay the ice on a piece of Styrofoam for easier work.

3. With a saw, remove any ice not required for subject.

4. Shape out the face and ears with chisels and use a die grinder for detail.

5. Shape out the tail and legs per illustration.

6. Smooth out and detail, accentuating the subject with a die grinder.

7. Finish the base as illustrated.

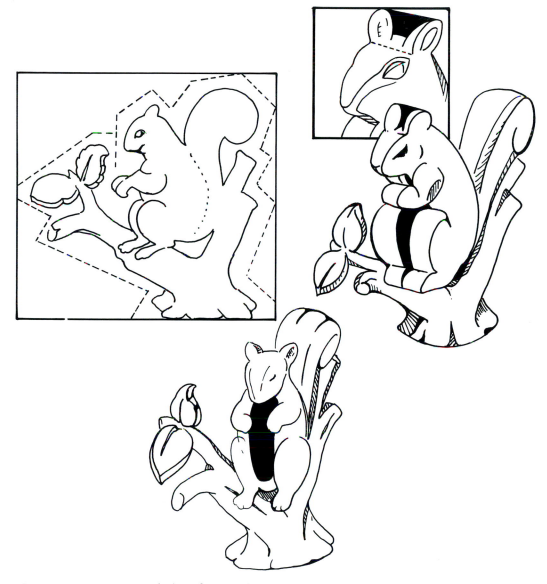

FIGURE 10–27 **Squirrel** Plans for templates and steps for carving.

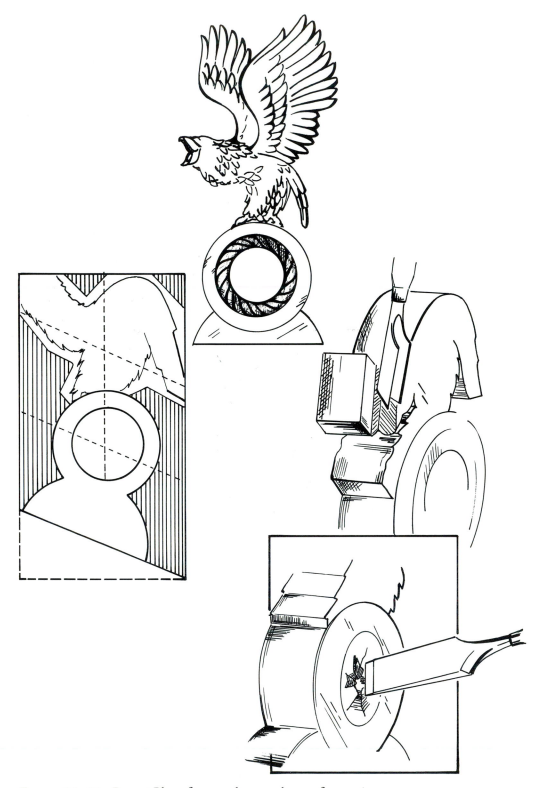

FIGURE 10–28 **Parrot** Plans for templates and steps for carving.

Parrot

1. Prepare your graph or stencil by following the illustrations provided. Use a model if available.

2. Lay the ice on a piece of Styrofoam for easier work. Wings are made from separate pieces of ice.

3. With a saw, remove any ice not required. As shown on Figure 10–27, notch the body where the wings need to be inserted. The notch must be large enough to accommodate the pegs carved at the ends of the wings. The more exactly they dovetail, the better the bond.

4. Shape out the head and beak with chisels, using a die grinder for detail.

5. Shape out the tail and legs as shown on the illustration.

6. Smooth out and detail, accentuating the subject with a die grinder.

7. Finish the base as illustrated.

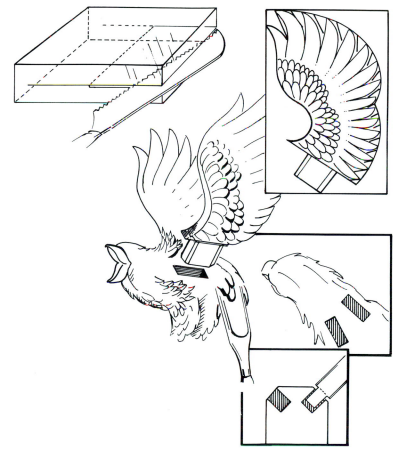

FIGURE 10–29 Parrot Plan for parrot-wing template and instructions for assembly.

Swordfish

1. Prepare your graph or stencil by following the illustrations provided. Use a model if available.

2. Lay the ice on a piece of Styrofoam for easier work.

3. With a saw, remove any ice not required.

4. Shape out the head and fins with chisels, using a die grinder for detail.

5. Shape out the tail as shown on the illustration.

6. Smooth out and detail, accentuating the subject with a die grinder.

7. Finish the base as illustrated.

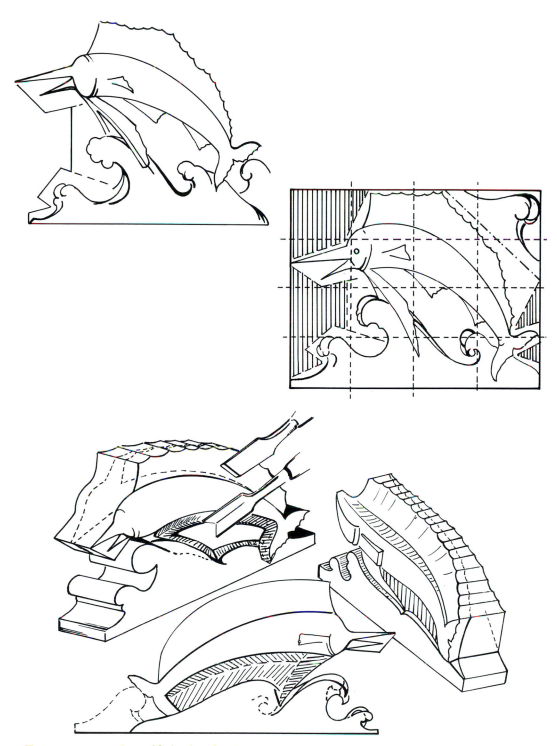

FIGURE 10–30 Swordfish Plan for the carving template and steps for carving.

Peacock

1. Prepare your graph or stencil by following the illustrations provided. Use a model if available.

2. Lay the ice on a piece of Styrofoam for easier work.

3. With a saw, remove any ice not required. Notch and groove ice as indicated in the illustration to ensure the successful final assembly of the carving.

4. Shape out the head and beak with chisels, using a die grinder for detail.

5. Shape out the tail and legs per illustration.

6. Smooth out and detail, accentuating the subject with a die grinder.

7. Finish the base as illustrated.

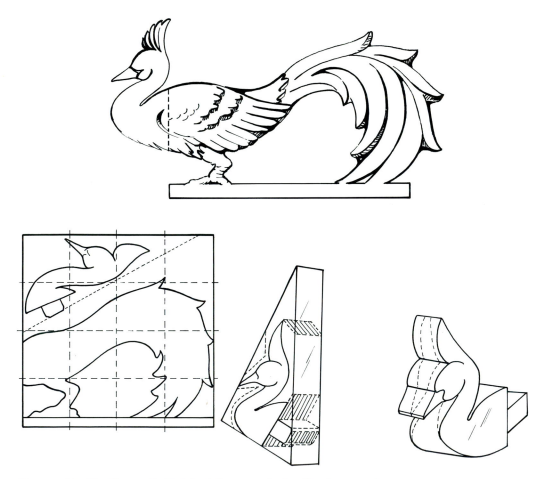

FIGURE 10–31 Peacock Finished figure and plan for the template.

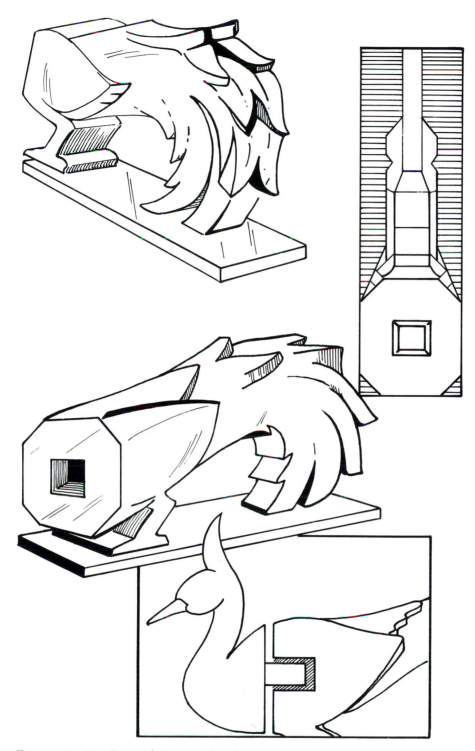

FIGURE 10–32 **Peacock** Base in detail.

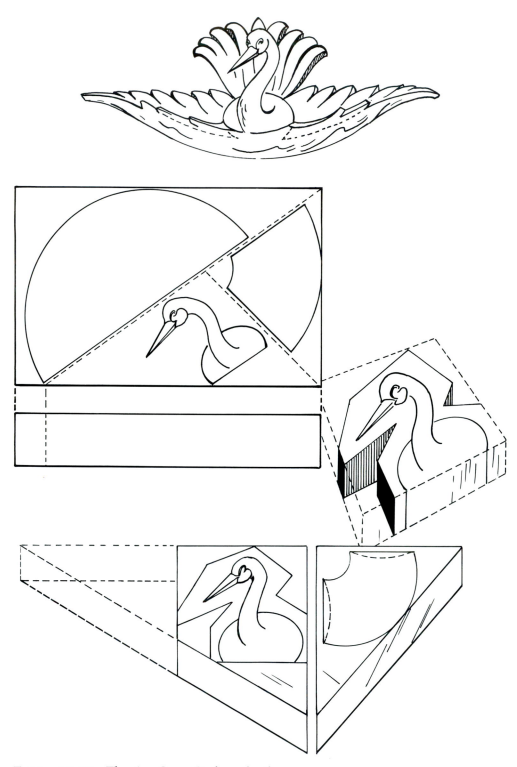

FIGURE 10–33   **Floating Swan** Body and tail.

Floating Swan

1. Prepare your graph or stencil by following the illustrations provided. Use a model if available.

2. Lay the ice on a piece of Styrofoam for easier work.

3. Study the diagram and illustration carefully before starting this carving. Remove with a saw any ice not required.

4. Shape out the face with chisels, using a die grinder for detail.

5. Shape out the tail as shown in the illustration.

6. Smooth out and detail, accentuating the subject with a die grinder.

7. Finish the base as illustrated.

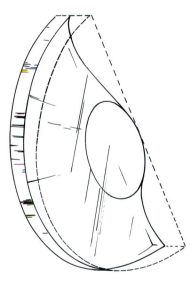

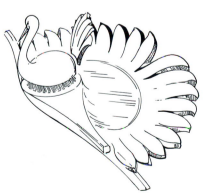

FIGURE 10–34 Floating Swan Base and final assembly.

FIGURE 10–35 *Photo and carving provided by Steve Rose.*

Swan

1. Make your template from the graph and scribe it onto the ice block.

2. With a large saw, make incisions on the upper part of the wings. With a shaver, remove all the excess ice from the upper part of the head and neck. Also using a large saw, cut down from the top, dividing the ice into thirds. This will bring out the center section that is used for the head and neck.

3. Remove the outer sides of the ice at a 45° angle, leaving the center exposed. With the ice chipper, shape the beak, head, and neck. Since this is the most fragile part of the swan, you should finish it first.

4. Next, silhouette the swan's body with the shaver. Now bring out the wings and body, using the shaver and a small pruning saw. Carve feathers on the wings and tail.

5. With a 1-inch chisel, bore holes at 45° angles for the eyes. Insert aluminum foil or large ripe olives. When well done, the finished swan should be graceful and suitable for many occasions.

FIGURE 10–36 Swan Ice block showing a plan for the carving template.

Kissing Swans

1. Prepare your graph or stencil following illustration provided. Use a model if available.

2. Lay the ice on a piece of Styrofoam for easier work.

3. With a saw, remove any ice not required.

4. Shape out the tail and wings per illustration.

5. Smooth out and detail, accentuating the subject with a die grinder.

6. Finish the base as illustrated.

FIGURE 10–37 *Photo and carving provided by Steve Rose.*

FIGURE 10–38 Kissing Swans Ice block showing a plan for the carving template.

FIGURE 10–39   *Photo and carving provided by Steve Rose.*

Twin Fish

1. Prepare your graph or stencil by following the illustrations provided. Use a model if available.

2. Lay the ice on a piece of Styrofoam for easier work.

3. With a saw, remove any ice not required.

4. Shape out the head and gills with chisels and use a die grinder for detail.

5. Smooth out and detail, accentuating the subject with a die grinder.

6. Finish the base as illustrated.

FIGURE 10–40 Twin Fish Plans for the figure and base carving templates: two blocks of ice.

FIGURE 10–41 *Photo and carving provided by Steve Rose.*

Love Birds on a Heart

1. Prepare your graph or stencil by following the illustrations provided. Use a model if available.

2. Lay the ice on a piece of Styrofoam for easier work.

3. With a saw, remove any ice not required.

4. Shape out the face with chisels and use the die grinder for detail.

5. Shape out the tail and beaks as shown in the illustration.

6. Smooth out and detail, accentuating the subject with a die grinder.

7. Finish the base as illustrated.

FIGURE 10–42 **Love Birds on a Heart** Plan for the carving template.

Basket

1. Using a cardboard pattern, scribe the outline of the basket onto the block of ice.

2. Shave away all ice not covered by the basket pattern, leaving a silhouette of the basket.

3. Saw away the front and back, leaving the center portion for a handle.

4. Using a shaver, remove the ice from the inside of the basket handle.

5. Shape the base of the basket and shave the handle for a rounded effect.

6. Dig out a well in the base of the basket, leaving chips to hold flowers, fruits, or beverages, as desired, and score the outside of the ice with a chisel to give a woven effect.

FIGURE 10–43   *Photo and carving provided by Steve Rose.*

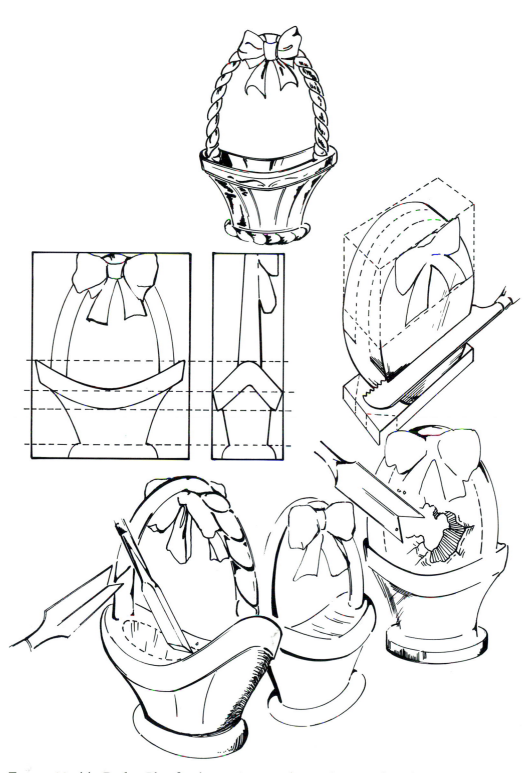

FIGURE 10–44 Basket Plan for the carving template and stages of production.

Fan Centerpiece

This unusual fan background won a gold medal at the 1988 Culinary Competition in Frankfurt, Germany. It was designed by Daniel Hugelier, who provided the photo and design for the book.

1. Cut blocks of ice, as illustrated, leaving two half blocks.

2. Split each section into two pieces diagonally.

3. Assembly a piece of cut ice on each side of the fan. Work the other pieces progressively toward the center. Precision cutting of the ice is of utmost importance to get the correct design and fit.

4. With chisels or a die grinder, create the prism effect to capture the lighting.

FIGURE 10–45 The finished **Fan Centerpiece**.

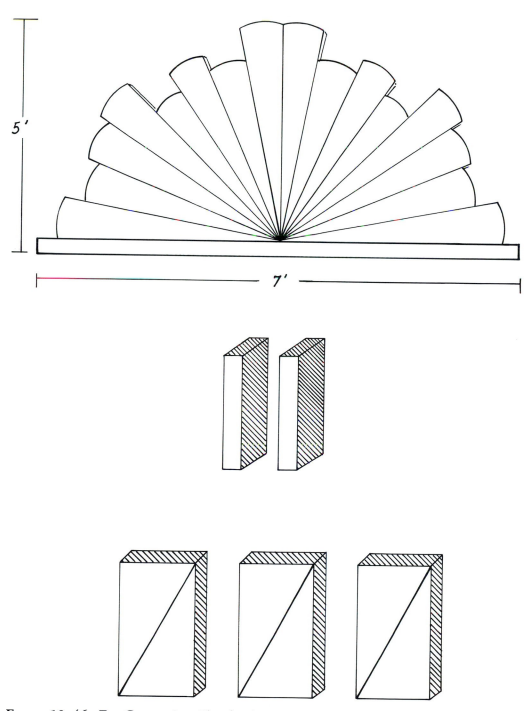

FIGURE 10–46   Fan Centerpiece Plan for the template and instructions for cutting the ice block.

Linked Chain

This very unique and interesting Linked Chain carving was presented to me by a former student and current instructor at The Culinary Institute of America, Michael D'Amore, with a note reading:

> Presented to Joseph Amendola during his 36th year reception at The Culinary Institute of America. "Thank you, Joseph Amendola, for linking us with your past."

As this carving is rather detailed and challenging, I recommend practicing with a piece of Styrofoam before attempting this in ice. Keep in mind that ice is brittle. Carefully follow these directions on how to cut, trim and release each individual link. Study the illustrations carefully before carving.

1. Use a full block of ice. Lay out the cuts as shown in part A of Figure 10–47.

2. With chain saw, make vertical cuts. These cuts go all the way through the ice.

3. Remove V notch from top and bottom of ice block (part B)

4. Part C shows horizontal cuts. Cut only halfway through the ice on solid lines. CAUTION!! Do no cut further than halfway through or the opposite link will be damaged.

5. If all is correct at this point, the top view along with the front and back view of the ice block will be as shown in part D and end view part E.

6. You are now ready to make the separation of links as shown in part F. Starting on one side, separate and shape each link while carefully cushioning them to prevent breakage. Half the links can be completed before loosening the links on the other side of block. It will require a second person to handle each side of the completed chain.

7. Display in an outstretched manner as shown in top illustration.

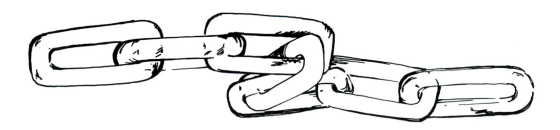

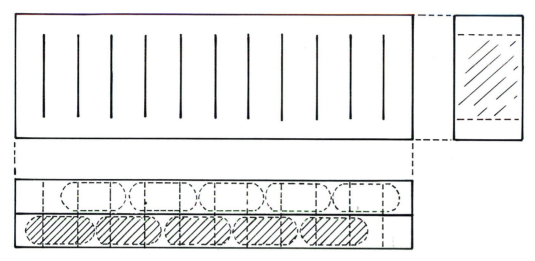

PART A

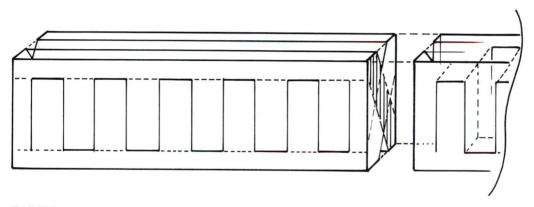

PART B

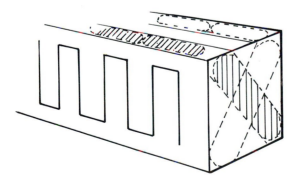

PART C

FIGURE 10–47 Linked Chain Plans for the carving templates.

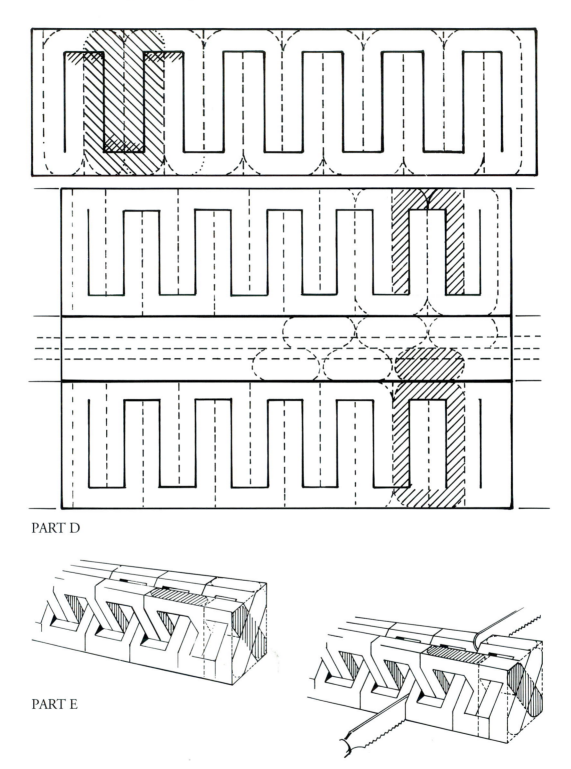

PART D

PART E

PART F

FIGURE 10–48   Steps for carving the linked chain.

Man Wrestling a Marlin

This carving was carved by Takeo Okamoto of Anchorage, Alaska, and was the gold medal winner of the international ice carving competition in March 1993.

It was carved from three 3,000-pound blocks of lake-harvested ice.

FIGURE 10–49 Man Wrestling a Marlin Stacked ice blocks bonding together before the sculpture is begun.

FIGURE 10–50 Carved body shown before extensions are added.

FIGURE 10–51   Finished figure with ice extensions—tail, leg, and other details.

Ice Block with Photo

This ice block with photo was presented at the 1993 2nd Annual Joe Amendola Golf Tournament Reception.

In this photo, professional Ice Carver Kanzo Tomori is shaking hands with Joe Amendola; in the background is an ice block with photo of Joe Amendola carving a swan in 1957.

This is just another of the many ideas for ice carvers to use.

The photos in this book were provided by Steve Rose of Ice Effects, Incorporated.

Steve has captured such titles as International Team Grand Champion and the United States Singles Grand Champion of Ice Sculpture.

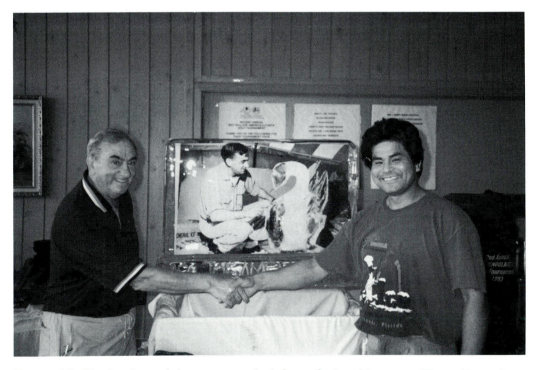

FIGURE 10–52 Joe Amendola appears at the left, professional ice carver Kanzo Tomori at the right.

Ice Castle

Perhaps the largest ice carving in the United States, this ice castle was carved and constructed for the 1993 American Culinary Federation Annual Convention at the Marriott World Hotel in Orlando, Florida. The project director was Kanzo Tomori, and the executive chef was Bernd Mueller, both of the Marriott World Hotel.

This carving measured 40 feet long and 25 feet high, with a skating rink in front large enough to accommodate three skaters. The castle required 250 blocks of ice, each $10 \times 20 \times 48$ inches and weighing 400 pounds, as well as 250 pounds of dry ice.

The project was completed by five carvers, two of whom were master ice carvers from Japan. It required eleven twelve-hour days, plus nine hours, to assemble this masterpiece.

FIGURE 10–53 Ice Castle carved by five ice carvers. Supervised by Executive Chef Yuki Iijima.

FIGURE 10–54   Cupid

The following ice sculptures were all carved and photographed by Steve Rose.

FIGURE 10–55   Easter Rabbit with Basket

FIGURE 10–56 Golfer

FIGURE 10–57 Chef's Bust

FIGURE 10–58   Antique Car

FIGURE 10–59   Mermaid with Shell

FIGURE 10–60   Horse and Carriage

FIGURE 10–61   Carousel

FIGURE 10–62   Dragon

FIGURE 10–63   Wild Geese